Why you'll want this book!

1. You want to exceed your current performance level

2. You want more time off with your family

3. You want more higher quality customers

4. You want to sell more products at a higher margin.

5. You want a better, faster way to sell

6. You want more customers for life

7. You want a different and better life style

8. You want to be the best you can be

9. You want more for your family

10. You want more ...

    And it can be yours with the information and insights in this book!

The Selling Gap
Selling Strategies for the 21st Century

By Harlan Goerger and Greg Deal

Copyright 2007
All Rights Reserved

ISBN 978-1-60461-248-6

Published by Deal Goerger Group
PO Box 5161
Fargo, ND 58105
701-799-1972
www.thesellinggap.com

Editor, Roxane Salonen
Fargo, ND
rbsalonen@cableone.net

Acknowledgements

A book such as this does not fly off the press without a great degree of assistance along the way. We, as Co-Authors, must acknowledge certain individuals that have helped us as we pursued this massive endeavor called writing a book.

(Harlan) I must acknowledge my family. They have provided a joy that can only come from those close to you. So thanks to Patrick, Nikki, Beth and the grandkids who always provide a smile. To Gwen, the Red Head, who has put up with me through the good and bad, providing a sense of humor and stability to my life.

Several experts have helped me to gain a greater understanding of this material. This allowed the development of several new concepts and strategies in this book. So thanks to Dr. Kevin Hogan and Dr. Eric Knowles.

Thanks to my Co-author Greg Deal and his belief in what we are doing, his support and his unending enthusiasm.

To all the customer past and present and the lessons they have taught me about people, communications and selling. Without those experiences this book would be hollow.

Harlan Goerger

(Greg) First off, a big thank you goes out to my wife Joan, for sticking with me during this venture. I couldn't have done it without you. There aren't many angels like you in the world, thanks for being mine.

I have been blessed with many great mentors in my life.

My first real sales job was selling a Live Bottom Asphalt trailer designed and built by a small regional company called Red River Manufacturing. I owe a debt of gratitude to the owners, Steve Danovic, and his now deceased partner Duane Lee. It was here that I came to learn all the aspects of marketing, sales and most importantly building solid relationships.

I still remember the excitement of my first large sale. It was Steve Danovic that brought me gently back to earth when he said "You sold him once, he's a customer, can you sell him again, now he's a client. What you want in your career is lots of clients, as they turn into friends".

I remember being a wide-eyed North Dakota farm boy rolling into Texas with that new product from Red River Manufacturing. Tom Dowdle took me under his wing, building on my strengths as an eager salesperson. His influence has a lot to do with the success I am today.

Thank you, Tom, for being a friend, and mentor for over 20 years.

Thanks to my Co-author Harlan Goerger. It is refreshing to find a kindred soul. It remains our belief that we must take care of the customer's needs, putting our product on the shelf until we find that need. Once the client sees the value, price is rarely an obstacle. Thanks Harlan, for being a friend, partner, teacher.

Thanks to Dr. Kevin Hogan, for teaching me how to build my influence and persuasion skills through your instruction. Your instructive tools such as the Inner Circle and the weekly Coffee newsletter were an incredible asset to me. This book is possible because of your teaching.

Greg Deal

A special thank you goes out to Dawn Koranda for producing the graphic art for the front and back cover.

Your friendship is greatly appreciated.

Last, but by no means the least, our very capable editor of this book, Roxane Salonen. With your writing and story telling experience, you were able to take our gibberish and make sense out of it. You did a wonderful job and your patience is commendable. Thank you.

Harlan Goerger & Greg Deal

Table of Contents

ACKNOWLEDGEMENTS 5

TABLE OF CONTENTS 7

SECTION 1: INTRODUCTION 1

PART I: STRATEGIES 3
PART II: WHAT IS SALES? 9

SECTION 2: PROSPECTING STRATEGIES 15

PART I: FINDING THE CUSTOMER (TARGET MARKET) 15
PART II: GETTING TO THE CUSTOMER (PROSPECTING) 23

SECTION 3: ENGAGEMENT STRATEGIES 35

PART I: THE BUYING PROCESS 35
PART 2: THE REVERSE ENGINEERING STRATEGY 41
PART 3: ENGAGEMENT STRATEGIES 53

SECTION 4: THE DISCOVERY STEP 59

PART I: BUYING GAP STRATEGY 59
PART II: SOCRATIC QUESTIONING STRATEGIES 67
PART III: FIVE LEVELS OF QUESTIONING STRATEGY 75

SECTION 5: RECOMMENDATION AND AGREEMENT 99

PART I: CONCEPTUAL AGREEMENT STRATEGY 99
PART II: RECOMMENDATION STRATEGIES 103
PART III: TRIAL QUESTIONS 107
PART IV: MOTIVATIONAL STRATEGIES 109
PART V: AGREEMENT STRATEGIES 113

SECTION 6: RESISTANCE AND OBJECTIONS 117

PART I: SIX-STEP STRATEGY FOR OBJECTIONS 117

SECTION 7: PERSONAL POWER 137

PART I: SELF-PERCEPTION STRATEGY 137
PART II: SELF-PERCEPTION MAKEUP 141
PART III: STRATEGIES IN CREATING A NEW SELF-PERCEPTION 153

SECTION 8: TYING IT ALL UP 161

A BIT ABOUT HARLAN & GREG 163

BIBLIOGRAPHY 165

CONTACT US: 169

Section 1: Introduction

With this book in hand, you have positioned yourself as a professional who is willing to be forward-thinking and grow toward continued success.

As a professional in the sales industry, you already have discovered the need to continually develop your skills and understanding in order to stay ahead of the competition. We are confident the principles in this book will move you closer toward your business goals in a rather dramatic way.

What you will find here are competitive-edge strategies that have been proven time and again to work, and work well. By the time you've internalized the concepts introduced, you will have discovered an approach that will carry you into a higher level of functioning with a far greater chance of success.

Some of the concepts outlined might be familiar to you. Others will introduce new strategies that have come forth from the latest research on persuasion and influence. These undoubtedly will be of immense value to you as a professional.

We have worked hard to keep out the fluff and in its place offer solid, understandable strategies that are easily applied. After all, you value your time and seek results.

This book is laid out in such a way that each section builds on the next. However, if certain areas intrigue you, skip ahead and read them first. Then return to previous sections to retrieve background information. There is no right or wrong way to read this book; just dig in.

For the sake of simplicity, throughout much of this book Harlan will be speaking, even though Greg has contributed to and experienced all of the ideas behind these concepts. Together, we've formulated our thoughts, presenting them to you as one person.

Part I:
Strategies

Travel now to ancient Scotland, where a general chooses a battle strategy using the fastest chariots to fight the Roman invaders. The fast chariots work in a circular pattern and continually pick up tired or wounded warriors and replace them with fresh ones. The strategy has worked exceptionally well in the past and has driven stronger and larger enemies back.

The Romans, on the other hand, use more discipline and employ several strategies. One surrounds the chariots, disabling them, and soon the Scots are defeated to the last warrior.

You may question what an ancient Scottish battle has to do with your business. Just because a current strategy works today doesn't mean it will be effective tomorrow, nor does it ensure that the competition doesn't have a better strategy.

When the word *strategy* is mentioned, reactions are mixed. Some respond with an air of understanding and approval, while others say, "Huh?!"

It is important to define *strategy*, since it is so central a theme in the Outcome Based Thinking approach that will unfold in future chapters.

Let's begin with some dictionary definitions. *Strategy* can mean:

1. Planning in any field: a carefully devised *plan of action* to achieve a goal, or the *art of developing or carrying out such a plan.*
2. Military planning of war: the *science or art* of planning and conducting a war or a military campaign.
3. Biology *adaptation* important to evolutionary success: in evolutionary theory, a behavior, structure or other *adaptation that improves viability.*

(Source: encarta.msn/dictionary)

I've emphasized certain words within those definitions to highlight how the word *strategy* will be used in this material.

- **A plan of action:** Planning is part of or the result of a strategy.
- **The art of developing or carrying out such a plan:** Many times we put together a plan only to find out, when the plan hits a glitch, that we've overlooked one or more essential components. A *strategy* is a broad approach that encompasses varied information.
- **Science or art:** A good strategist has experience in viewing a situation in a multi-dimensional way. This gives them the insight into possible barriers, walls or opportunities others might miss.
- **Adaptation that improves viability:** Strategies should allow flexibility so one can move with the situation and adapt to changes as they occur or are going to occur.

How might this be different than the planning you are now doing?

Far too many business and salespeople react to a given situation rather than think it through strategically. This may be due to workload or the intense, daily focus needed to run a business, as exemplified by the phrase,

"I need to spend more time *on* my business rather than *in* my business."

Here is a quick example of how a strategy can replace a reactionary plan to change a situation dramatically:

Recently I asked a young man beginning our program to name a specific objective he would like to accomplish by the end of the five-week session. His objective was clear: to have his long-distance girlfriend move closer to him.

I helped him apply Outcome Based Thinking to create a strategy that would be valuable to both of them regardless of the result. He devised a plan and determined what tools would work best to help *his girlfriend* through the decision process. He knew it might mean the end of the relationship, but that if he approached her with a thoughtful strategy his chances of obtaining a "yes" would be much greater.

Even before the course's end he happily announced his engagement and shared that his girlfriend had decided to move near him.

This client agreed that having a strategy enabled him to view, act and communicate differently than he had been and that the outcome was the right choice for *both* of them. Prior to applying Outcome Based Thinking, he had been focusing only on what *he* wanted and how he might get it. He had been reacting to the situation rather than viewing it as a multi-dimensional situation. Once his view and focus changed, his intent and tools also changed, which made all the difference in the outcome.

During the Cold War the United States chose treaty negotiation as its strategy to improve tensions with the Soviet Union. Numerous treaties were signed and subsequently disregarded. Enter President Ronald Reagan, who noted that the Russians were bankrupt and suggested that outspending them into oblivion could change the course of the Cold War. A few years later, the Soviet Union was completely bankrupt and disbanded.

How was Reagan's strategy different than those before him?

If you look at history you can see how most negative events took years if not decades to change. And yet many times the change came, and often it occurred quickly when the strategy changed. President Reagan had a very different view of the situation and approached it in a very different way then his predecessors; thus, the desired outcome happened, and fairly rapidly.

What about your approaches to situations? Are you more *reactive* or *strategic*?

Here are a few more examples of how strategies can be applied:

- One of our advisors keeps things secret. He is excellent at creating a desire in a potential client by withholding certain details. He perpetuates a great mystery and curiosity that causes the person with whom he is talking to want what he offers.

- Another advisor offers something of value for free to potential clients to initiate reciprocity, which quickly moves into the sharing and building of a partnership. He fosters trust and value upfront to draw in clients.

Both of these individuals have been successful at getting results for their clients. Both employ strategies that, although different, work.

Here are a few more:

- One bank employs an expert in each field such as mortgage, finance, investment, etc. The customer visits several experts in the process of doing his or her banking. This creates confidence in the customer because of the expertise, although it discourages the building of relationships.

- Another bank has its personal bankers handle everything from checking to investments. The customer works with one person and can create a long-term relationship with that person.

Both banks are growing and gaining market shares. How are their strategies different?

By now you can see the difference between a *strategy* and a *reactionary plan*.

When being introduced to the concept of thinking more strategically, people often say they do not have time for it, yet they have time to make more phone calls, lose more sales and work longer hours.

Do you happen to know anyone like this?

As we proceed thorough this book, you will see the word *strategy* many times. You also will see the words *plan* and *tools*. The three fit together in this way:

1. A *strategy* is developed based on research, understanding and questioning the outcomes.
2. An *action plan* is put together to carry out the *strategy*.
3. The *tools* needed are brought into the *plan*.
4. The *plan* is carried out and measured for effectiveness.
5. The *plan* is successful or is altered on the go to make it successful.

You may not use every tool provided in this book. After assessing each situation you will use those that fit your strategy and plan based on your prospective client's needs.

Part II:
What is *sales*?

"I'll tell you one thing for sure; the only things worth learning are the things you learn after you know it all." -- Harry Truman

There are three sales people in the same market selling a very similar competitive product. One earns $30,000 a year; another, $70,000 a year; and the third pulls in $210,000 a year. How can the difference in performance from three competitors whose offices are within six blocks of each other be so vast?

What does one have over the others to cause a 700-percent difference in earnings?

Over the following chapters we will work with strategies and skills that can create the above difference. Because the foundation of everything in this book is understanding what sales is and is not, let's get a good understanding of this foundation.

A man wants to buy a new television set. He goes to the Internet to peruse the latest information, reads the newspaper and other ads, and consults the *Consumers Report,* finally deciding he wants a Panasonic TH 58PX60U - 58" plasma TV.

He notes a sale ad at the local store and goes to check it out. Once there he finds the television section, locates the model of choice and looks around for a salesperson to help him buy it.

The salesperson appears, asks what he wants and gets a warehouse employee to get it for them while they take care of the paperwork. The man goes home with his new television and the salesperson gets credit for such a great sale.

Who sold who in this example? Did the buyer depend upon the salesperson for information, direction, negotiations, applications or any other duties a sales person may have? Did the salesperson employ any type of strategy or skill?

I would say the sales person acted as an "order taker" and the customer sold himself on what he wanted.

Today thousands of buyers are walking through stores, surfing the web and scouring many sources of information, looking for someone to sell them something. The issue seems to be that *sales* and *selling* are very misunderstood by most of the general public and, unfortunately, by many business professionals.

We have been taught through myths, legends and sales training that the product/service is the main attraction to the customer. Is it?

Let's re-examine the television example. Why do we want a television? Does it provide us entertainment, current information, an escape from our stress, a bond among our family and friends, serve as a status symbol, or is it just another appliance or piece of furniture? Our buyer obviously was looking for some very specific features in his television as he conducted his research. Did the salesperson have any idea why the buyer wanted the television? Probably not, but he got credit for the sale.

So what is *sales*, really? In ancient times, before money came into being, business was conducted by bartering.

Your strategy would be to trade something you had for something you or someone else wanted. Merchants would trade with craftsman in one region and then trade those wares for other items from other craftsman. They would continue to trade goods back and forth based on the needs of another party.

As the merchant's trade area grew and included different countries, the need for a common currency with an established value was required; thus, money was created. Bartering ceased to be the preferred method to exchange value when fulfilling the needs of the customer with a particular product or service.

It's the same today; *sales* is discovering needs and wants; then determining the best way to fill that need. Sophisticated marketing helps to create awareness and may even create a market for a new concept, but marketing alone does not always create and fill the need.

There is an adage that goes, "Everyone is tuned into one radio station, WIIFM, What's In It For Me?" If this is true, salespeople need to focus on, "What's In It For Them?" Professional sales should focus on *customer needs*, not the product itself. In other words, people buy what the product *does*, not the product itself.

Let's repeat that: *People buy what the product does, not the product itself!*

A line we use in our training is, "If it could be done better, faster and cheaper, would you buy it?" Most would say "yes."

Let's apply this to some of the items sold daily. Take the automobile. If we had something that was better, moved you faster and cost you less without compromising your independence, would you buy it?

If you could buy a product that allowed better, faster and cheaper communications, would you discard your phone?

We could take anything in the market today and apply the question, and most would say "yes."

Why? They receive the benefits of the original product with more speed, better quality and lower investment. So, do buyers want the product or what the product does for them?

What strategies help salespeople remove themselves from the category of "order takers" into the arena of "professional salesperson?" That's what this book is about. More specifically, we call it, *The Reversed Engineered Strategies of Selling* or "*The Selling Gap*".

You most likely have heard, "As a man thinketh, so shall he be." This is the central idea of being a professional salesperson. The professional is always focused on what the customer is looking for in their product, not the product itself.

Determining the customer's needs is the foundation of *The Selling Gap*. Instead of looking at the product we first must look at the customer and his or her situation through their eyes.

In order to accomplish this, the professional uses an inquisitive and investigative strategy with the customer. Well-planned questions uncover the needs and desires of the customer before any product is even presented.

How is this different from the typical approach?

Many companies place the training focus on the product and product knowledge. This is commonly known as the "features and benefits" of the product being sold.

It begins with the reason why customers should buy, at least according to the company's perspective. The company sends out the salesperson and he talks about the product and why the prospective customer should buy it.

These salespeople are not taught to consider it from the customer's viewpoint. It is not surprising that many new salespeople view the sales profession as being difficult.

Let's reverse that view and focus on what the customer is seeing, wanting and needing. But one must be cautious and not assume the customer is seeing their situation the same as the salesperson might. Once the salesperson has the customer's view they can see how their product fits the customer and present it as a solution rather than just a product.

How does this differ from your current strategy?

How, exactly, does *Reverse Engineered Sales* describe selling? There are six key ideas from which the professional functions when looking at selling:

1. A sale is a higher level of communication than our normal daily conversations. Communications in sales needs to be planned, focused and purposeful. It also needs to be friendly, open and sincere. Much of the communication is determined by the customer and how the salesperson responds to that communication.

2. This higher communication also is very visual and body language becomes more important than the words used. The professional is aware of this higher level of communication and is continually working on these skills.

3. *Reverse Engineered Sales* is results-driven, not product-centered. The professional does not push product for the sake of product. The emphasis is on needs, desires and solutions for the customer.

4. The professional is always determining the needs, problems, challenges and opportunities from the customer's viewpoint. This way the salesperson

becomes a friend, confidant and, most important, a consultant of the customer.

5. The professional always provides solutions or helps to create opportunities for the customer. This task becomes easy once the customer's wants and needs have been revealed.

6. The professional may understand the customer better than the customer understands himself. You may ask how this can be, but this is what counselors and coaches do everyday.

7. The professional creates opportunities and solutions for his customer before the customer is aware of the need.

By now you realize we put the customer's view as more important than the product or product knowledge. This is true, but product knowledge is needed to formulate the communications, approach and solutions. What becomes most challenging is not letting the product knowledge become an obstacle to providing the customer with his wants or needs.

The following pages will provide you with strategies that utilize your product knowledge in a different way so you can obtain a better outcome for you and your customer.

Three key concepts to remember:

1. *Sales* is a higher level of communication.

2. The customer buys for his or her reasons, not the salesperson's.

3. Many salespeople let their product get in the way of solving the customer's needs.

Section 2: Prospecting Strategies

Part I:
Finding the Customer
(Target Market)

Have you ever watched a fly in a window buzz away trying to get out, using all its energy only to end up totally exhausted and defeated at the end of the day?

The whole time the fly is struggling, only a couple feet away is an open door and victory.

When prospecting, how many times have you felt like the fly?

> *"Hey John, what have you got going this weekend?"* Rob asks.

> *"I've got paper work and several customers to see yet on Saturday. I need to get my numbers for the month!"* John replies. *"How are your numbers looking?"*

> *"Oh I hit the quota on Monday. I've got a golf date this afternoon and am heading to the beach for the weekend."*

> *"That's NOT FAIR! We both make the same commission. How come you always seem to be golfing or going to beach?"*

"I felt the same way until I changed my daily prospecting strategy and started thinking differently about how to acquire business."

"Okay, I'm listening. Tell me more."

Is your prospecting strategy a barrier to your success or an asset?

Prospecting plays a primary role in sales success and strategy determines what tools are required to carry out prospecting successfully. Focusing on a particular customer makes it easier to focus our choice of tools and how we might apply them.

This chapter's purpose is to help you create a productive prospecting strategy that gives you a steady steam of highly qualified prospects. With this highly focused pipeline of prospects the balance of the selling strategies also can be more focused and effective.

There is a saying that goes, "Nothing happens until something is sold," and I believe it is true.

No company or organization would exist for long without some type of customer or sale. A sale provides the cash for product, production, research, support operations, marketing and all other activities that keep the organization going.

How many companies say they are selling too much and have to cut sales?

What are some of the steps we need to ensure that we have customers purchasing our product or service?

In order to zero in on our customer we should ask some or all of the following questions:

- Do we think our target customer is everyone out there? Not only is this unrealistic, but it's also too broad to be effective as we zero in on our true target market.

- Are we looking at a vertical market in a specific industry, such as auto, computer or medical? Or is it a horizontal market (geographic area) of a certain size and all types of business?
- How large or small is our customer base? Where are they located? How do we make our product or service known to them?
- Finally, but no less important, *what do they need*?

All these questions and more need to be addressed before we can "target" our market.

I spent time consulting an industrial company with varying sizes and types of customers, from individual farmers to large multinational companies.

We developed a system of classifying customers as "A," "B" or "C" based on the *potential* purchase capacity of those individuals. Interestingly, all three categories ended up with the same total dollar potential. Here's why:

- The "A" group comprised the large industrial plants that could spend millions every year.
- The "B" group consisted of the mid-size to smaller plants that would spend thousands every year.
- This left the "C" group, those smaller plants and farmers that would spend hundreds in a year.

Of course, the "A" group had the smallest number of customers but also had some large hurdles to overcome. One main hurdle was "preferred vendors" that had the computer capability that allowed their buyers direct access to inventories and ordering online.

The company simply did not have the capital or capacity to provide such a service at that time. Should they invest thousands of dollars to be competitive at a reduced profit margin?

Or should the strategy concentrate more on the "B" customers that the "preferred vendors" were not as active with?

We chose to increase our efforts with the "B" group while continuing to work with the companies in the "A" group with whom we had relationships. The result was a 400-percent growth in three years.

In other words, know your strengths and match them with the market strategy you're pursuing.

We conducted a marketing campaign using advertising and mailings to the "C" group, which was an inexpensive means to produce awareness of our offerings to a low-volume market.

It's important to note that all three categories had equal potential for sales. When we looked at the number of contacts in each category it was staggering how many were in the "C" group.

The main problem with the "C" group was the time it would take making sales calls to get the same dollar volume as the "B" or "A" groups. The "A" group gave the challenge of more competitors asking for the same business at greatly reduced margins.

What we did see is that many of the "A" competitors were ignoring the "B" group where our company could receive a better margin on the effort put forth.

Your strategy will cause you to focus on your target. The clearer the vision of your target, the easier it is to find your customer.

Perhaps you've had the experience of seeing something for the first time, like a car, dress or new item. You buy it and the first time you drive it, wear it or use it you see several other people with the same car, dress or item.

You didn't notice them before because you were not focused. Your purchase focused your awareness and now you see all the other people with the same thing.

It's the same with our target market: the more clearly we can describe it, the better chance we have of finding customers who are a match for our product.

Once our team understood how to clearly define their target customer, our productivity, sales volume and profit margins went up.

If you're not focused you can miss what's right under your nose. Here's an example of becoming aware of what's available in your market.

I was conducting sales training with a mixed group of salespeople from different industries. One car salesman wasn't getting the target market concept. I asked him who he would love to have as his customers, to describe them, to explain where they lived and why he would want them as customers.

His description covered the younger to middle-age, upward mobile families with two working professionals, a couple of kids and a specific income level. It was obvious he could target very specific community areas that were occupied by his desired customers.

Once he did the work in developing his target account, he devised several marketing plans to contact this group and win their business. His sales increased by 100 percent in the next several months with half the effort.

Target marketing works!

As you look at defining your "target," use your *Reverse Engineered* results to help determine what the perfect customer might look like. Some helpful questions to ask:

- What industry or customer type would most benefit from the results of my product?
- Who has the most buying potential?
- Who is the easiest to reach?
- What will my sales cycle time be on average?
- What will the cost be per sales call?
- Where would the best profit margins be?
- How might my current company limit the potential?
- What strengths could my company provide that fit well?

Once the target customer is well-defined it is possible to narrow the list of "everybody" down to those who have the most sales and profit potential fitting your situation. Then, with a well-developed strategy, you can plan your attack and be very productive while increasing your success ratio. You can begin drawing in business that has been there all the time but only recently became clear. This business stands out like that new car or outfit did when you first bought it.

The following page provides a sample profile sheet. Use it as a starting point to develop your own target customer profile.

Target Customer Profile

Company name:
Address:
Type of business:
Major products/services:
Number and type of locations:
Subsidiary of:
Annual sales volume:
Type of ownership:
Subsidiary names:
Major Executives:
      CEO:
      President:
      VP's:
      Key contacts:
            Phone #s:
            Fax #s:
            E-mails:
            Key contacts outside company:
            Friends with:
            Personality type:
            Main likes:
            Main dislikes:
            Associations/club memberships:
            Birthday/anniversary:
            Time with company:

Current supplies/vendors:
Criteria for choosing suppliers:
Major past changes:
Major future changes:
Company decision process:
Future growth plans:
Current purchase volume from you:
Potential purchase volume from you:
Current opportunities for you:

Future opportunities for you:

Part II:
Getting to the Customer
(Prospecting)

"Courage is resistance to fear, mastery of fear; not the absence of fear."
Mark Twain

I recently did a research paper on a local company that has been very successful in capturing over 70 percent of their market and has claimed the highest profit-level of all the companies' multiple locations. The sales manager felt that 40 percent of the salespersons' time and effort needed to be on prospecting.

Note that even though the company has captured 70 percent of the market, it still emphasizes new accounts. Their success has been accomplished by using the sales process outlined in future chapters.

So let's assume you have your target market defined and it provides you a good picture of your prospects. What strategy will you use to contact them, uncover their needs and recommend a solution?

Let me emphasize there is no magic formula other than a well-executed plan with multiple approaches. Many times I have seen salespeople depend on one method of prospecting and wonder why they don't succeed.

Let's look at several sources in prospecting that have proven effective.

Referrals make up the most powerful tool in prospecting. People tend to know and work with others like them and they likely have established some level of trust between them. This gives the salesperson a higher quality "in" to the referral and usually reduces the time from introduction to close significantly.

Zig Ziglar has said, "Timid salespeople raise skinny kids!" We need to ask for referrals on every call, whether we have a sale or not. If you have developed a trust level, most people will help you out. The key is asking in the right way.

Oftentimes salespeople do not always know how to ask effectively. "Do you know of anyone else who might be interested?" is usually not the most useful approach. It is too broad and undefined, leaving an unclear picture of who would make a good fit for a certain product or service in the customer's mind.

Relying on the Reversed Engineered sales planning in conjunction with a Target Market plan will lead to a more valuable description of those with whom we want to do business. By providing our customers with this visual they can pinpoint others who might be a match.

Here is one way it might work:

> *"Mr. Jones, we have invested some time in understanding your organization's needs and how addressing those needs can move you forward. You obviously know many businesses that face similar challenges and are looking for solutions. I'll describe some characteristics for you.*
>
> *Please tell me who comes to mind.*
>
> *These organizations have leaders that look for change, their organizations are similar in size to yours, are located with in 200 miles of here, are in a*

*competitive industry, need the culture change you
seek, may have or are going to merge soon and are
open to new ideas.*

*Which of your suppliers, associates or neighbors
might fit this?"*

As the names emerge, clarify the information, contacts
and perceived needs of the new prospect. Once you have
the information, ask for permission to use their name on
the referral.

Asking the customer to call the referral while you are
there and set up an appointment for you is another tactic
that has proven to be effective. If the customer knows
the referral well they can get through and you have a
very solid "in" to a new prospect. This also solidifies your
relationship with your current customer, and makes them
more likely to do business with you.

How can they refuse now?

Remember, timid sales people = skinny kids!

Once you've obtained the referral, how might you best
use it to secure an appointment? Talking in the
customer's language and using a *value or problem solving
statement*, which will be addressed soon, will be a great
help. It might look something like this:

*"Ms. Everet, I was talking with Mr. Jones at XYZ
Company about reducing its loss of production during
its merger and conversion.*

*He mentioned your organization is going though a
similar situation and may benefit as they have by
reducing the conversion time significantly. We have
several ideas on how this may work.*

*When would you be available next week to look at
how we accomplish this?"*

I spent time working with a company that had a salesman by the name of Leroy. Leroy had been selling a life insurance product for several years and had never made a cold call after the first few months. He was a master at getting referrals and always had someone to call on. I never had to wonder why he was always on the "top producers" list.

Newspapers and Magazines can provide another helpful prospecting tool.

Consider the following. Earl, a seller of sales training, was reading a local business magazine and came across an article on a company being chastised about their inability to sell their great ideas.

Not wasting a minute, Earl called the company and got the chief-executive officer on the phone. He mentioned the article, and in a very short time an appointment was scheduled. The company registered several people into his sales program. I wonder how many other sales trainers read the same article?

Once the target market has been defined, it is helpful to determine which newspapers and magazines will offer insight into these target markets. Just knowing who is who in a particular market can provide great credibility. The local library is a great place to find magazines and industry-specific information.

Vendors and Suppliers are also key. If you are working with an organization that supplies others, many of their customers may fit your profile. It is in the vendor's interest to keep their customers profitable.

Years ago I operated an agricultural business. We sold seed, chemicals and agricultural services. Most of our growers were very profitable, but farming can be a fickle industry.

utilize your *Reverse Engineered Information* in creating your statement.

Let's say you're in the office-equipment business and sell copiers. Do you say you're in the copier sales business? Or would this be better: "I am with SAE Inc. and we specialize in freeing up your organization for productive work." Which would engage the other person more effectively? Make sure to use the customer's language. Then follow up with open questions that help qualify potential customers developed with our *Reverse Engineered Information*.

Keep it brief and light, and exchange cards and information. Unless a prospect wants to spend more time, five minutes is a long enough time at a network event. Remember, the prospect is looking for customers as well.

At any type of formal event such as a Chamber of Commerce After-Hours program, be sure to follow basic etiquette and manners. Are you there to eat a plate full of food or meet people? Are you there to pass the gossip or leave a good impression? Are you there to connect with old buddies or meet new potential clients and future friends? Be positive, enthusiastic, open and brief so you can impress, converse and meet as many new people as possible.

Don't forget to network on a personal level as well. Recently I contacted a former participant in our sales training who had just gotten married and moved back to our area. We had coffee and talked about family, homes, recent job changes and the future. Along with giving me several names of key people to contact in several companies, he also committed to helping me connect with the new company for which he was working. Because of this contact, I ended up making another connection that ended in the closing of a large, annual contract.

A couple months later I met with the president of his new employer and closed a nice piece of business. I had tried several times to get something going with both of these organizations previously with no luck. And now I offer his name whenever I find people needing his service. What comes around goes around.

Annual Reports and Prospectus also can help. If you are working with publicly traded organizations, obtaining copies of their annual reports, which are available to anyone, can be useful. Ask your broker to get a copy or use the local library or internet. These reports list all the key players, divisions and departments and their functions, those in charge, the goals and objectives for the coming year and a review of the previous year. All or any of this could be useful to your business.

You might, for example, consider analyzing each executive's report based on what you perceive to be their priorities, and determine how you would prepare a presentation for them. After reviewing several of these for the same company, take a look at the differences in each proposal. This exercise can offer valuable insight into the personalities, priorities, values and motives of each executive.

Lists of different types are available from many sources. They can be very broad or very specific. I generally ask for a specific organizational size and location when obtaining lists. Most of the information is updated but in our highly mobile society things change daily. You can buy lists naming the chief executive officer, number of employees, sales volumes, type of industry, type of product and almost any other information needed. If you do get erroneous information, just ask for the current information. Most receptionists are accustomed to providing updates.

Current Customers: Consider whether current customers use all of your services and products, and whether you might be overlooking a possible sale.

The life insurance industry gives annual awards to its top producers. One such producer shared how his business doubled in a year even though he never made a "cold call." He simply went to his files and determined what he could do to get 100 percent of the possible business from his existing customer list.

Likewise, list all the services and products you provide and set them against each customer. What are your current customers now using and what could they use? When you find a fit, go get the business!

Methods and sources of leads abound. Keeping your pipeline full is a matter of tapping into those methods and lead sources. You can have the greatest product and the most fantastic presentation on earth, but it is futile if you have no one to hear about what you have to offer. Prospecting and lead generation needs to be an integral part of your sales plan and requires some level of activity every single day.

With a pipeline full of pre-qualified prospects, the rest of the selling strategies can be focused and become even more effective for you.

In sum, here are the "musts" in the area of prospects, targets, marketing and qualifying:

1. Have a well-defined description of your target customer.

2. Focus will save you time and increase your production.

3. There are many ways to find and qualify customers.

4. A good marketing strategy uses many methods at the same time.

"Develop the courage to make decisions. That's the most important quality in a good leader. Don't fall victim to the "ready-aim-aim-aim syndrome." You must be willing to fire!" - T. Boone Pickens

Section 3: Engagement Strategies

Part I:
The Buying Process

Notice: *"If you want to sell your product to our company, be sure your product is accompanied by a plan which will so help our business that we will be more anxious to buy than you are to sell!"* Unknown

Psychologists have studied many aspects of the human psyche over the years, including behavior patterns, attitudes, decision-making, buying habits, parenting approaches and more.

From this, we have learned that all behavior, including buying, follows a process of some type. And when a subject moves through the "process," the end results are very predictable and very repeatable. This bears repeating: *When a subject moves through the "process," the end results are very predictable and very repeatable.*

In this section we will provide you with a quick overview of the "selling/buying" process, its psychology and its steps. Included are short insights into each aspect of the steps to help you internalize the concepts.

We will assume the proven strategy that our selling will be approached from the buyer's prospective, and that product knowledge along with well-placed questions will help us to find that viewpoint. But how do we bring the buyer from "hello" to purchase?

To do this as professional salespeople, we need to know the process and how to lead our customers through it. Let's return to our first example with the television:

A) The buyer becomes interested in a new television. *Engagement* is the first step in the process.

B) Before deciding on a purchase, the buyer considers certain needs he would like to fulfill, although he may not be fully aware of them all. He searches the Internet, reads appropriate books and advertisements and determines a buyer criterion (desired features). The buyer is now in the *Discovery* stage, the second stage of the process.

C) Armed with the buying criterion, the buyer begins to select the model that fits his list. He has entered the third stage, or *Recommendation*.

D) At this point the buyer's motivation is based on value or price because no one has helped him develop any emotional reasons to move forward. Looking over the ads, the buyer finds the model on sale and prepares to get into action. *Motivation* is the fourth step and involves emotion.

E) Our buyer goes to the store to find someone to help him finalize the purchase, which is the *Agreement,* or fifth, step.

F) The salesperson (acting in the role of order-taker) helps the buyer through the *Agreement* step but most likely skips the sixth step, which is *Follow-up* after the purchase.

Suppose a quality salesperson met this buyer and helped them through the process in an effective way. Would they buy sooner? Would they be willing to do it now? Would they be willing to pay more? Absolutely!

Now some of you might be saying, "This is manipulative selling," or, "This is con-artist stuff," or some other non-gratifying thought. Be assured, every successful salesperson uses this process in one form or another.

Let's take another look at our television example:

- Do we know what the buyer wanted other than a television?
- Do we know the desired features and why?
- Do we know whether the buyer assumed to understand the features? If so, might that assumption be in error?
- Do we have any idea what motivated the purchase process or the purchase itself?
- What if the buyer is in error in understanding the features and buys the wrong model for his needs?

If the television should go home and the buyer soon discovers it does not fill his needs, we will end up with an unhappy customer.

We must return to the buyer's perspective. A professional makes his or her recommendations based on what will best fit the buyer's needs. Does this seem manipulative?

The *Webster's Dictionary* definitions of *manipulation* include: 1) To treat or operate manually or mechanically, especially with skill; 2) To manage skillfully; 3) To control or change by artful means to achieve a desired outcome; and 4) To change or affect for improvement.

Before we dive into the process itself, one more element must be addressed: *emotion*. Some find this to be a very nasty word that is best avoided. They often assume that all choices and decisions are logical.

The next time your favorite old song comes on the radio, see if you can prevent an emotional response. My past wife, Joyce, and I had a favorite song, *Color My World*, by the band Chicago. Whenever I hear it, it always seems to bring back some level of feelings. Think of songs, movies or stories that evoke feelings in you. Emotions do affect and motivate us.

When it comes to our decision to purchase something, both logic and emotion come into play. One saying goes like this: "Buy on emotion and justify with logic." Almost all of the choices and decisions we make in life are emotionally driven. We just happen to spend a lot of time justifying them with logic later on.

In one of our sales programs we gave a presentation to several salespeople from a high-tech software company. They were a very bright team with a lot of product knowledge and confidence. When I introduced the idea of emotional buying, they fought it. It just didn't make logical sense to them.

I then challenged them to try it on the big sales call they were to make later in the week. They agreed to plan it into their call to see what might happen. During the next session they told me the results were unbelievable; the call had gone extremely well and a sale was secured with what seemed to be much less effort than earlier attempts. They noted that they accomplished in one call what would have taken several calls with their former approach: a purchase order had been obtained practically on the spot. Emotion has now become a permanent part of their software sales.

As we progress through this buying process, we'll need to be aware of the need to look for emotional cues as well as the logical facts to determine what our buyer wants and needs.

The following sections will provide you with the tools to not only discover these emotional aspects but also how to utilize them in a way that will turn out the desired results.

"I have always assumed that it is my job to provide the seeds and the customer's job to provide the manure. If we put together what each of us has to offer, we can make something grow." – Ira Ellentahal

In summary, the buying process steps include:

Engagement
Discovery
Recommendation
Motivation
Agreement
Follow-up

New to Sales? Want to get a faster start and hit the ground running! **Quick Start Sales 101** will get you there!

Go to www.thesellinggap.com/products.html. Indicate you have "The Selling Gap" book and get online coaching FREE!

Part 2:
The *Reverse Engineering* Strategy

In September of 1953, at the conclusion of the Korean War, a young 21-year-old North Korean pilot took off and flew south. The personnel at Kimpo Air Base were wide-eyed as the sought-after Mig 15 landed in the South Korean base. Sick and tired of the "Red Deceit," Senior Lieutenant Kum Sok No had defected, unaware of the $100,000 reward to anyone who could provide a complete Mig 15 to the United Nations or United States Military. The Mig 15 was flown to Wright-Patterson Air Force Base and completely and painstakingly disassembled.

Reverse Engineering is the process of taking something that is complete and disassembling it to find out how it really works. The Mig 15 was the most advanced jet fighter at that time and the U.S. Air Force was struggling to catch up. The unexpected delivery of this Mig 15 pushed the United States ahead and helped its dominance in the Vietnam air war.

The United States was willing to spend $100,000, well over $1 million by today's dollar, to acquire a Mig 15 in 1953 only to tear it apart. What might be your gain as a sales professional to disassemble your product?

Encouraging salespeople to look at their product in terms of results the customer receives has been a constant challenge over the years. Yes, product knowledge is very important, but it can get in the way of what the customer really wants.

In the attempt to find ways to help salespeople translate their product into results, the *Reverse Engineered* strategy came into being.

Aaron, an engineer, and I were talking over lunch one day about how to translate a highly complicated product into terms high-level investors could understand. Naturally he was focused on the product and its technology.

Out came the paper napkin and we started breaking down the product into factual information and then determining what that might mean to high-level investors – in *their* terms.

Suddenly the light bulb came on and Aaron understood. Very quickly he was able to take the factual information and translate it into results the investors could relate to and would want to hear.

Reverse Engineering the product from a sales presentation standpoint was born.

Since then I have refined the process, applied it in my company and tested it with others. And now I share it with you in the hopes you will transform your business through implementing it.

It is interesting how this process can be applied not only to product but to situations as well. I have analyzed various scenarios using the *Reverse Engineering* tool and found all types of different views and approaches because of its application.

Reverse Engineering is taking an item apart to see how it is made and how it interacts with other components, and then determining the potential final results the user could experience. Oftentimes this leads to salespeople changing their perception of their product and interacting with their customers differently. This translates into more sales and less time invested.

Consider the following as you determine how much of an investment you are willing to make to master this process:

- It will take time and effort for you to work a product through *Reverse Engineering* – at least initially.
- It will require you to think differently about your product.
- It will force you to create a different type of questioning than what you have employed in the past.
- It very likely will result in your obtaining extra commissions and income from thinking and selling more effectively.

In other words, a little time investment up front very likely will pay off big in the end.

Reverse Engineering now becomes a bridge to cross the chasm that often separates the product from the users' results.

By absorbing and practicing the following material you will master the strategy and change your communications and selling results.

Reverse Engineering

Your **product** with facts, features and benefits

The **results** your customer really buys

Your bridge to success!

Let's return to an idea brought forth earlier that customers buy the *results* of your product, not the product. In focusing on the results that come from the product, it becomes easier to develop questions to bring out the pertinent information relating to the customer's desires. Once that information has been obtained, it is easier to determine a fit and then present our product as the solution.

To get started we need to take the product/service apart and break it down to its facts, elements, features and functions.

1) *Facts, elements, features and functions* are the physical aspects of a product, such as its size, controls, color, options and other things you can generally touch and feel. Keep in mind that even intangibles have facts and features.

2) Next we need to determine what the potential benefits are from each of these facts, elements, features and functions. There can be multiple benefits from any given fact.

3) Finally we determine all the potential results that the customer and end user could potentially experience from these benefits. Once we have this we can work backwards from our results (*reverse engineer*) to create our questions.

When breaking down our product to its **factual components**, its facts/functions/features, we look at characteristics that are not opinions and must be provable by an outside means.

Let's use a Styrofoam cup for an example. Here are its **factual components**:
- Made of Styrofoam
- 16-ounce capacity
- Stackable

The **potential benefits** of a Styrofoam cup are that it:
- Keeps things warm,
- Is lightweight,
- Can be manufactured easily and
- Is disposable.

Each benefit can have many different **potential results** for our customers. Take the benefit of "keeps things warm." Our potential results could be:
- Less waste,
- Less employee time per customer,
- Satisfied customers and
- A better company image.

Likewise, the benefit of "light weight" can have potential results of:
- Fewer Worker Compensation problems due to employee injury,
- Virtually anyone on staff can handle the product,
- A quicker response to customers from staff and
- Less staff needed per shift.

With the potential results listed, we can now focus on whether this fits our customer. Because we have the answer, it becomes easier to create the open question to uncover which result is important to our particular customer. We then concentrate on the *results*, not the product, and develop *open-ended questions* that help us understand the *real results* wanted by our customer and fit the product to that result.

Take something familiar such as the television. What are some of the results of having a television in your home? Information, weather, sports, news, local information, education, entertainment, world views, relaxing time, time with family, the gang over for the game, escape from the daily grind, conversation with friends and co-workers, new ideas and much more. Hopefully you can relate to one or more of these ideas.

Let's use one of the examples and *reverse engineer* it.

Fact	Function/Benefit (What it Provides)	Results
Daily Weather Report	Planning Information	Helps me plan my weekend
Warns of bad weather	Gives me a secure feeling	Helps me protect my family

Now take the results and design questions to bring out the information from the customer's viewpoint:
- *"How important is the weather report to you and why?"*
- *"What type of impact does the weather report have on your planning?"*
- *"Of all the information reports available, how does weather reporting rank?"*

How does this type of questioning differ from what you might use? Would you ask, *"Do you watch the weather?"* What is your next question? Will it be difficult to engage this prospect in a conversation?

By *Reverse Engineering* we can get closer to the true viewpoint of our customer faster and more effectively. We also can get more information about their values, decision-making and motivations.

Let's try another one: life insurance. First we must determine the facts, elements, features and functions of the product. Life insurance provides money, hedges against taxes, provides security for family, saves assets, provides a savings or investment fund, and increases net worth.

Here are more examples of *Reverse Engineering*:

Fact	Function/Benefit (What it Provides)	Results
Increased Net Worth	Immediate Estate	Financial Security for Self
	Assists me in getting Financing	Improves my balance sheet

The *Reverse Engineered* questions might look something like this:
- *"What net worth would you need to feel financially secure?"*
- *"How would an improved balance sheet change your situation?"*
- *"What would your banker need to see to get faster approvals?"*

Here's one more product example: computer printer. Its facts, elements, features and functions are that it provides a hard copy, is less costly than a printing shop, is convenient, provides company image, promotes communications, can provide fun, provides flexibility and saves time.

Fact	Function/Benefit (What It Provides)	Results
Quality Image	Company Image	Communicates progressiveness to customers
Provides Flexibility	Cuts Response Time	Instant response to customers

Our *Reverse Engineered* questions might be:

- *"What would you like to see different in your response time and image to customers?"*
- *"What is the image you would like your customers to have of your organization?"*
- *"How would quicker and clearer internal communications affect your people?"*

The strategy of starting from the customer's view and creating open questions based on the results of our products allows us to create more powerful and directed questions. These types of questions will provide the salesperson with a clear view of what the customer sees as their greatest need.

Also note that many of these questions have little to do with the product but they bring out the bigger picture; i.e., the customer's values and how he or she makes decisions based on their motives. This will turn out greater opportunities for both the customer and the salesperson because they are seeing the bigger picture, not just the product application.

Reverse Engineering will be referenced in every chapter and section of this book from here on out. Through using this approach, you will begin to see the sale in a new light, and in turn, the strategy and tools you use will change and be more effective. As such, it is important to gain as strong an understanding of this concept as possible to maximize absorption of the rest of the material. If more time is needed to internalize the concept, do take the time to review until your understanding of it is firm. Doing so could make all the difference in the level of your success

A form used to develop these questions follows on the next page:

Product: **Ceramic Coffee Cup**

Fact	Benefits	Possible Results of Benefit	Reverse Engineered Question
Has a handle	Provides convenience	Customer is more relaxed	How important is convenience to your customers?
	Reasonable way to hold it	Fewer accidents	What would a way of holding a hot drink without burning your hands mean to you?
	Safety	No injured customers	In your view, how important is your customer's safety when dining?
	Offers a way to hang and store	Saves staff time	What would a quick and effective storage method do for your efficiency?
	Adds style and image	Customers/staff see us as classy	How do you see your image and how important is it to your business?
Holds 12 ounces of liquid	Provides container for liquid	Reduce delivery time of product	If you could individualize your servings, what would it mean to you?
	Reduces inventory needed	Provides more convince to customers/staff	If you could provide a repeatable service to your customers, what would it do for you?
	Provides flexibility for staff	Cuts staff time to serve customer	How could you use a multiple function item such as this?
Is ceramic	Almost lifelong usage	Reduces costs	What is the life on your current cups? What if you could increase it?
	Can hold hot - cold	Saves storage space	If you could use one system for both hot and cold liquids, what would it do for you?
	Reduces stains	Reduces inventory replacement	If you could eliminate stains on your cups, what would it mean to you?
	Reusable	Reduces cost of operation	Of what importance is minimizing waste to your operation?
	Can be reused infinite times	Improves profit picture	In what way would an infinite recyclable system affect your profit?

As you can see, this process can take a simple product such as a coffee cup and gives it a very different meaning. Does this differ from the average approach such as: *"We also have coffee cups in different colors and shapes. Would you be interested in any?"*

Check your grasp of the *Reverse Engineering* process:

1. Take a product and come up with as many fact/feature/functions as you can and list them in the first column.

2. Determine all the related benefits in the second column across from the fact/feature/functions.

3. Now ask yourself what results this may provide your customer from their view. Think broader than your product and ask, "How does this result really affect my customer?"

4. Finally, start developing your *Reverse Engineered* questions based on this broader effect.

Open questions will be much more effective at gaining more information quickly. These questions generally use "how, what, why or tell me." We will go more in depth on this in our *Mastering Questions* section later on.

A quick review of key points in the *Reverse Engineering* process:
1. Focus on the **potential results** of the product.

2. Create **open questions** to determine the customer's desired results.

3. By following the above, **greater insight** into new and different applications of the product will be gained more quickly.

Sales Cycles

Before we move any further, it's important to pause to make note of the different sales cycles that exist for different products and services.

A television can be sold very quickly in one encounter or sales call, while a large engineered project or complex process may take several calls over several months. The same process is used but the steps may be spread out over time or you may take the customer through the steps several times at each stage of the sale.

Part 3:
Engagement Strategies

The phone rings, you answer it, the voice on the other end asks for so-and-so, mispronouncing your name. You think, *Telemarketer – hang up*! But when you call a prospective customer for an appointment, is your strategy any more engaging?

Remember, the buyer does not want our product but the results of the product. So the purpose of the *Engagement Step* is to positively engage the customer based on what can be provided if given the opportunity. This step does not include the sale, but the attempt at a first *yes*. We need to determine what will be most likely to lead to that.

Corporate executives have an average of 56 hours of work in front of them any give time of day. When we call such a person and they pick up the phone, are they thinking, *"Great, a sales person with all the answers?"* Not likely. So we must disengage them from what they were doing and thinking and reengage them into what we can do for them.

Talking about a product has been proven very ineffective in engaging others. As soon as a product is mentioned it gives the customer something to reject, and the "reactance" or push-back begins because they do not want to buy or be sold something. They may not be connecting their problems with your solution yet, so there is no reason to say *yes*. Our goal is to reduce or eliminate resistance.

The *Reverse Engineering* process helps determine some possible results. This combined with pre-approach information can provide us with a very strong *Value or Problem Solving Statement*.

These statements cut right to the core of what the customer is looking for and dealing with. A strong *Value or Problem Solving Statement* needs to be in a language the customer understands. If a customer hears an issue that is important to them, they have a difficult time rejecting it.

Some examples of *Value or Problem Solving Statement*:

In researching your company I see you recently merged with another group and have (1) changed the organization significantly. We have had great results in other organizations in (2) reducing their time in getting to full productivity after a major merger, many times by half the time they thought it would take. This of course means time and cost savings for you and your organization. To make this happen for you we (3) need to meet and determine what steps would work for you.

A recent study of your industry has indicated a (1) severe turn-down in the future due to new technologies. I assume you are aware of this and are looking for possible solutions. We have (2) several new ideas on how to capitalize on these new technologies and maintain your market share. (3) We will need to meet to discuss these ideas in full. Next Tuesday is open for me.

Recently I talked with several of your sales executives and they said there are (1) internal strife issues blocking customer-service productivity. We have had great results in (2) reducing and eliminating such issues and increasing productivity in similar organizations. When, next week, (3) are you available to discuss this issue?

In viewing your organization I've discovered you (1) release several new products a year. We have been able to (2) reduce the time and cost of new market introductions by as much as half. I have several ideas that could work. (3) What time on Tuesday could we meet to discuss these ideas?

As a local business owner you are probably dealing with (1) cash-flow issues and looking for solutions that can help you grow at the same time. We have (2) created several programs that have assisted small business in maximizing their cash flow and also helped improve their business. (3) Let's take ten minutes to see how these ideas may work for you.

In breaking down these statements we find one component provides a (1) potential problem that the buyer can relate to, followed by a (2) statement of solution. The statement of solution should contain a statistical value such as "by half" or "several ideas" or "eliminate," all of which add value to the statement. The language used needs to be direct, avoiding "maybe" or "possibly" or other words that leave an impression of uncertainty. And always end the *Value or Problem Statement* with a (3) call to action.

The above examples can be used as appointment-getting tools and also as a tool to start the sales interview. The key to the *Value or Problem Statement* is to view it from the customer's perspective, use their language and request action.

Another tool is the *Problem or Results Oriented Question*. This poses the problem or results in an open, broad-question format to get the customer into a short dialog. This short dialog can create interest based on the possible result instead of the product. Many *Reverse Engineered Questions* work well in this application.

Remember, your objective is to get into the next step called *Discovery* or setting the appointment.

For example:

> "Suppose you could prevent your sales people from leaving thousands of dollars on the table. How would it affect your company?"

> "If you could get an additional $5,000 cash flow per month from five feet of floor space, how would it change your monthly picture?"

> "What would a more efficient office operation mean to this organization?"

> "Let's assume your bank could do even more for you. What would you want and why?"

Remember, the purpose of the *Engagement* is to move the customer through the process. Get them disengaged and reengage them in a productive dialog.

Let's take this first step called *Engagement* and see how it would flow in a sales interview setting. We have made the appointment and are now in the customer's office.

The Engagement Step

This begins with a short introduction and beginning some small talk about the referral (if we used one), possibly about the ball game or another similar surface/personal question to break the ice and set the tone. The challenge is to remain in control of the initial conversation or it could take up all the allotted time. I have seen the discussion on the ball game, fishing trip or hunting adventure run 20 minutes or more.

We take control by asking the right question in an appropriate way:

"By the way, Mr. Jones, (referral) said this new merger was a very complex one and is proving to be very demanding. As I mentioned we have had great results in other organizations in reducing their time in getting to full productivity after a major merger, many times by half the time they thought it would take. This of course means time and cost savings for you and your organization." (Value or Problem Solving Statement)

Some other conversation-change words: *"Interesting. Have you considered...?" "Now that reminds me of..." "Oh, did you know..."*

A **bridge statement** would follow. Some examples: *"To better determine just how we can do the same for you I need some information, can I ask some questions?"* (This is called a *bridge question to Discovery*; it takes you from one step to the next step in a smooth, logical fashion).

It is also important to get permission to interview. I have seen this small item skipped and the *Discovery* stage suffers because the customer is unwilling to really open up. Asking permission seems to minimize this issue.

Another tool called the **credibility statement** can be added if needed in talking with new customers to add credibility and give them a better idea of who you are. After all, you have pre-approach information on them, but how many have information on you? The credibility statement involves a very brief overview of your company, product and results:

"Mr. Jones, our company, XYZ Inc, was established in 1985 by the same leadership we have today. We work with mid- to large-size organizations in addressing performance improvements in their personnel and have shown measurable results from 35 percent and up. Some organizations we have worked with are CCC Inc, BBB Inc and ZZZ Inc."

"Just a quick introduction, we are a fairly new organization but we have over 40 years of experience in the field. Several experienced people in the field felt they could do better for the customers and created our company DDD Inc. Our current customers are rating our service and results are as high as 9's and 10's. Here are some brief comments from them....

If needed some reference material such as letters or other credibility-building items can be added, but remember the word *brief*. The object of this step is to provide some level of comfort to a new prospect that has no idea of who you are. We generally use this before the *Bridge Question to Discovery*.

Note that the *Value or Problem Solving Statement* that was used to secure the appointment is repeated here to start the sales process. I always try to tie all the steps together with a common statement or issue. Using the statement also helps tell the customer it is time for business and gets them focused.

Section 4: The Discovery Step

Part I:
Buying Gap Strategy

Dan had been in sales about five years, and although he'd accomplished a lot, he felt that there was more to be gained if only he knew how. During one of our sessions we introduced Dan to the *Discovery* stage and the concept of the "Buying Gap." It wasn't long before something began stirring inside of Dan. A renewed energy and brightness showed in his eyes, as if a light bulb had been turned on in his brain.

Two weeks later Dan won the honor of the "best application report" for his company, and he shared with us how he'd done it. He'd simply jotted down the four steps we'd introduced to him, and then followed through. With every sales call he made during those next few weeks, he went through the steps, asking questions he'd never before attempted or even thought of attempting. The results: he began closing over 70 percent of all his calls, and by the end of the year he had more than doubled his sales volume.

The secret to Dan's success is no secret at all. You, too, can take advantage of the process that led to the astounding results Dan experienced in his work.

There are several names for this stage: the *Discovery* stage, the heart of the sale, or the interview phase. If you watch a highly skilled interviewer at work, it is as though they are in complete control, and the interviewee is at their mercy. It is amazing what a skilled interviewer can get high-profile people to say on television.

You have the same tools at your disposal, and you can use them with your customers if you plan and practice the process we are about to reveal.

First, it's important to understand the purpose of the *Discovery* step. In the first chapter we emphasized the point that our customers buy for their own personal reasons. We also stressed the idea that we need to know those reasons as well as the emotional motivations, values and decision process behind them.

In the second chapter we introduced *Reverse Engineering* with the purpose of viewing the product from the results it provides, not simply through the facts and features. The reality, as we now know, is that our customer buys the results.

If we can fix this information clearly in our mind as well as in our customer's, we will almost always be guaranteed a sale. Obtaining this mutual view of the customer's situation and motives is the purpose of the *Discovery* step.

Psychologists have shown that 70 to 80 percent of our population is visually-or image-oriented. This means their mind processes inputs such as words and numbers as images rather than words; very likely one of the reasons movies and television are so popular.

For example, which of the following creates a more vivid picture for you?

He sat in the chair, or

John sank deep into the soft green cushion of the overstuffed chair, putting his short body into an awkward, yet comfortable state.

If I say the word *fire* what happens in your mind? Do you see the word *fire* or do you see an image of flame, smoke, heat or something similar that signifies a fire for you?

What is happening to you emotionally in these previous examples? Do you feel a slight tug or twinge of emotion as you visualize the green chair or the image of fire?

The *Discovery* step should create a clear image for both the customer and salesperson as well as bring out the emotional aspects of that picture.

Making a list of what you will need to know about your customer in order to determine how your product will fit is an important step in the process. What criterion is necessary? What qualifying information will help?

We use a four-step process called *Buying Gap* in our interview questioning. This process is designed to help both the salesperson and customer see the same picture, even if the customer does not see it initially.

The steps include:

- **Current Situation**: We find out what is happening today, what things are working well, the culture of the company and personnel, how decisions are made, who makes the decisions and other pertinent information. We need the salesperson and the customer to create the same mental image of the current situation.

- **Future View:** This includes learning what they hope the future will look like, what goals and targets they need to hit in order to get there, what changes are planned, who will carry out those changes, and why they want those particular results. If the customer can visualize the future, many of the emotional or motivational aspects will start emerging. It also helps create a "buying gap" between where they are and where they want to be. This gap between the Current Situation and Future View helps to bring out their real issues so we can address them. Thus, the wider the "buying gap" the greater the potential for a sale.

- **Hurdles:** What has kept the customer from achieving the future view, what barriers (internal and exterior issues) need to be overcome, who is responsible for the success of these and what would happen or not happen if hurdles are not overcome? This can help provide accountability for the customer and allow them see the need sooner and attach them to their "fear of loss" or "promise of gain."

- **Rewards:** If the future view could be achieved, what is in it for them personally, as well as for the company, and who is rewarded and in what way? Why is this important, and to whom is it important? Both "reward of gain" and "fear or prevention of loss" can be rewards. What would happen for them if the "real issue" is dealt with?

As we move through this process, we will want to look for several items that provide us the keys to the customer's thinking.

These include *Results* (what the customer is looking for in our product, how they measure it, and why those results), *Criteria* (Are there certain facts or features they need, a specific size or speed, cost restrictions? And how do they determine which supplier to use?) and *Emotional Button*, which is the real key to faster and more profitable sales (the emotional motives of the buyer, which might include love of family, pride in work, ego, greed or the desire to make a difference and receive recognition).

Note: Money is *not* an emotion! Instead, look for what money will do for them and take them to the emotional level.

It's important to understand that as a salesperson we have two ears, two eyes and one mouth. Nature has a neat way of providing us the type and number of tools we need to be successful. Therefore we need to use our tools according to their numbers. In other words, we should listen twice as much as we talk and observe twice as much as we talk, or a ratio of 4:1.

In the first chapter, we discovered that seeing our product from the customer's view is the basis of sales, and product knowledge tends to get in our way when used incorrectly.

To bring all of these ideas together, it's essential to keep the product out of the interview and listen more than you talk. Our purpose is to gain a deeper understanding of the customer's emotional motivations so we can recommend the proper solution.

We believe a 20-minute interview means the customer talks for the first fifteen minutes. We tell all of our sales program participants to "Lock your product in the trunk!"

With this listening in mind, let's dissect this *Discovery Step* interview. We need to have *Reverse-Engineered* our product to develop fully effective questions. Many of the *Reverse Engineered* questions can be directly transferred to this step.

How many questions do we need to ask? As many well-planned questions as are needed to establish a clear picture in both the salesperson and customer's mind.

As you read the following dialog, notice that the product is not involved. Also note how the answers could provide clues to values, motivations and the decision-making process.

Also, as you think of how someone would answer these questions, be mindful of what type of picture if being formed in your mind.

In the *Current Situation* we want to get a clear picture of the customer's situation today. We also want to clarify that picture in the customer's mind. So let's continue with the company merger.

"Mr. Jones, could you give me a thumbnail review of this merger from your viewpoint?"

"Tell me about the people involved."

"You're indicating three different groups coming together. How would you describe the cultures of each group?"

"What type of time table was indicted in your plans for full integration of these groups?"

"What do you see as the main time user for yourself in this situation?"

"Do you have a current cost of turnover per employee, and if so what is it?"

In the *Future View* our objective is to create a clear view of the goals of the customer, even if they don't have a clear view. The clearer this view is and the more it contrasts with the Current Situation, the greater the "Buying Gap" and the greater the sale potential.

"Part of your purpose in merging was better efficiency. What levels of efficiency do you want in the next year and how will you measure it?"

"What are the plans and objectives that you put as your priorities for the next two years?"

"How do you see your department and position changing in the next two years? Why?"

"What other objectives may your organization have for you in the future?"

The *Hurdles* portion is to create a solid picture of what is preventing or could prevent the *Future View* from happening. This should create an awareness of what needs change as well as create a high value in the customer's favor for making a change.

"What do you see as the major obstacle in obtaining the efficiencies you want?"

"What is your plan to over come these obstacles?"

"What happens if the objectives are not met? How does that affect your goals?"

"How would increased turnover affect your projected outcome?"

Rewards should bring out the *Emotional Value* the customer has vested in the situation. Even the most stoic buyer has some emotional attachment.

"Mr. Jones, how will you be measured in this situation?"

"How will that affect your future?"

"How would a better outcome affect your personal goals?"

"What are some of your future goals?"

"What makes that so important to you?"

As one goes through the process, we recommend trying to do each step thoroughly before moving to the next. But many times cues and clues come up later, and moving back and forth through the four steps is acceptable as long as it is not confusing for either the customer or the salesperson.

Review the questions in the four-step example now. How many were open- type questions versus closed?
If the *Discovery Step* is done correctly and well, most sales can be closed at this point (*Agreement Step --* conceptual agreement). We will return to this soon.

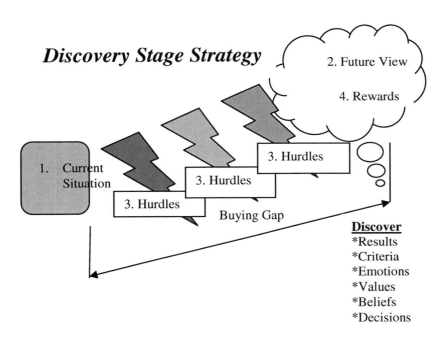

Discovery Stage Strategy

2. Future View

4. Rewards

1. Current Situation

3. Hurdles

3. Hurdles

3. Hurdles

Buying Gap

Discover
*Results
*Criteria
*Emotions
*Values
*Beliefs
*Decisions

Part II:
Socratic Questioning Strategies

"In the end, all business operations can be reduced to three words: people, product and profits. People come first." – Lee Iacocca

As you walk across the plaza with the warm sun on your face, you notice a short, rather shabby-looking man standing alone. He seems to be completely self-involved and talking to himself. Strangely, everyone seems to simply accept this behavior and continues on by.

After you've completed your shopping, you see him again in front of you. He very quickly engages you with a question and soon you find yourself compelled to discuss some current issues. You find him rather interesting and, curiously, you feel his questions probing around in your mind. After a time you part, but you find it strange how you seem to have a very different view of the topics you just discussed.

It is 450 B.C. and you have just met Socrates.

The ancient Greek philosopher, Socrates, has been called the Father of Modern Thinking. He even had a basic theory of the atom; it just took a couple thousand years for the proof to catch up.

His philosophy included the thought that all people are born with all the knowledge they need. It is getting out this "Truth" so they can see and use it that becomes the challenge. In order to do this "Truth," Socrates developed a system of questioning that guided his students though this process of discovering the knowledge within.

This method of answering a question with a question, utilizing open-type questions and using questions to guide another to a predetermined conclusion, is called the Socratic Method of questioning.

Today the best communicators, therapists, counselors and sales people rely on the Socratic Method. As sales professionals we need to be able to understand our customer's needs even if they do not. The ability to uncover those needs and guide our customers to a conclusion is the "higher level of communication" we have been working toward.

What makes the art of questioning so important in sales? Most people deal only with surface issues in their communications. I've found many times people who have known each other for years still do not know some basic things about one another.

This calls to mind Robert, his two brothers and their father. Every year the four of them would take a fishing trip together. They always enjoyed each other's company, and each would take turns telling exaggerated stories. Yet one year Robert realized most conversations focused on sports, fishing or some other standard topic. They didn't really know one another very well at all.

After going through our training and thereby coming to understand others at a deeper level, Robert decided to challenge his brothers. That year during the annual fishing trip, as they talked and joked, Robert began probing. The other three reacted in a stunned manner at first, but soon began to answer the questions. The fishing rods became secondary as the conversation began to go to a deeper level than it ever had before.

At times the conversation became very somber as one or the other disclosed their true feelings about certain situations they'd experienced. But as they discovered the finer points of each other, the conversation also turned truly joyful.

The four men returned home with a very different view and understanding of each other. "It was great!" Robert reported upon his return.

Think of a few of your close friends and customers, and in your mind, ask these questions about them:

- Do they know what motivates others in their lives?
- Do they know what they use as a reference for their decision-making?
- Do they know their business and personal goals?
- Do they know their values and how those values affect their thinking?

The science of questioning will undoubtedly take you to a new level of understanding and skill. If done well, it can not only improve your sales but your personal relationships as well. Many professionals who have taken the time and effort to master this material have found dramatic results in many areas of their lives.

In the pages that follow we will explore different levels of questioning, how to discover the type of information we are looking for, and then determining and building on that information.

This *must* become your way of thinking before the skill can be mastered. It will take time, effort and practice. But if you could double your income, productivity and performance tomorrow with the same effort and time you use today, would it be worth it?

The Four Types of Socratic Questioning

Students attending Socrates' school did not have books, but would engage in a continual dialog of questions and more questions until the answer could no longer be questioned. This is how one found their "Truth."

Most of what we know about Socrates was revealed through the writings of his students, such as Plato. As you review the plays of Shakespeare, the influence of Socrates comes through. Sigmund Freud found the Socratic Method a must in developing his psycho therapy, and modern salespeople utilize the Socratic Method to influence clients.

We break the method into four types or uses:

1. **Answer any question with another question.** This is one of the basic premises and keeps you in control of the conversation.

2. **Utilize open questions to discover values and beliefs.** Modern persuasion is based on understanding values and beliefs and either aligning with them or changing them.

3. **Frame questions to direct.** This is used to direct conversations and thinking in a predetermined direction.

4. **Frame question to overcome resistance.** This assists in overcoming resistance and gathering the true information about a given situation.

The **first type** of Socratic Questioning is perhaps the best known but most misunderstood. It is the answering of a question with a question.

Consider the following line of questioning:

"What would cause someone to do that?"

"Why do you think they would?" is the response

"Well, what would be your take?" the questioner asks back.

"I'm not sure. Your take on it is?" is the response

The above example represents a misinformed understanding of answering a question with a question. After about three rounds of such an exchange, each party is going to start getting red flowing up the neck and past the ears!

Instead, the questioner should end their response with a question that puts them back in control of the conversation and its direction. A conversation that employs the correct kind questioning might go something like this:

"What would cause someone to do that?" John asks.

"I have often wondered that myself. What insight might you have, John?" Bill asks.

"Personally I have very little, but a friend of mine indicated the behavior might come from conflicting drug usage," John answers

"That's interesting. What experiences are you aware of concerning this?" Bill asks.

"Oh, I really have no experiences or knowledge about it," John says.

"Well my mother had .... How does that relate to this situation in your view?" asks Bill.

"Wow! That sounds just like this situation. Maybe we should do the same thing," John suggests.

"I would agree. What would be your first step?" Bill inquires.

Who is in control of this conversation and its direction?

The key is to always end with a question that gives you control of the discussion, direction and content.

Practice this with a friend or associate. Start a conversation on any subject and see if you can each end your comments with an open question back to the other party. You may find it more challenging than you think.

The **second type** of Socratic Questioning is the use of broad, open questions. By using the words **how, why** and **what** we create an open type of questioning that requires a thinking response rather than a simple one-word answer.

In our training we do a simple test with our participants on their ability to continually ask open type questions. Most people put forth two or three of these types of questions in a row before slipping back to closed questions. Occasionally we get someone who can do 20 to 30 in a conversation.

How much more effective would your conversations and sales become if you were to use more open questions? We will be investing more time and examples of this in the next section.

The **third aspect** of Socratic Questioning is the re-framing of questions to direct or steer the conversation.

Let's say you are trying to persuade someone on a certain issue or want to find out a specific piece of information. By framing the question you can direct the type of answer you might get.

If we take an open question and add or delete given words, we change the direction of the question. It changes the image the other party may have in their mind.

Two monks were meeting in the hall.

"Good day, Brother John. You look a bit down in the mouth."

"Yes, Brother Mark. I just asked the Bishop if it was alright to smoke while I prayed, and he said, 'Absolutely not!' "

"That is interesting, Brother John, because just yesterday I asked the Bishop if it was alright to pray while I smoked, and he said, 'Sure!' "

Both monks asked basically the same thing, but each got a different response. How they framed their request made the difference. Consider the image each question creates in the Bishop's mind.

What would you have said?

By changing some words in the following question, how does it change the answer or direction?

If you were to make a change, how would you go about it?

If you were to start a change, how would you go about it?

If you wanted different results, how would you go about it?

If you wanted more results, how would the team go about it?

How does changing one word or phrase alter the answer you might receive?

The **fourth type** Socratic Questioning is reframing for correction. This tool is very useful when a direct question will most likely not get us the full or truthful answer. By framing our question in a way that causes the other party to correct us, we can oftentimes get the full story and information.

You most likely will need some level of information about the situation first to frame in this fashion. This utilizes our natural tendencies to correct errors others make.

Let's say you have several competitors that could be bidding against you. If you ask directly, "Who am I bidding against?" the answer may be evasive and defensive, such as, "We really don't give out that information."

But you know that one of the possible vendors is much smaller and may not be able to meet the specifications, so you could frame your question this way: "I understand that TBY Corp. is looking at bidding on this. Do you have any insight into this?"

A response to that kind of question might be something like this: "Oh, they're too small for this project. You'll be bidding against MBN and Tri-Print."

Yes it can be that simple. People do respond to this framing surprisingly well. They not only feel compelled to correct you, but to provide even more information. Correcting someone is an inherent reaction we all have in such situations.

In the next section you'll find more examples of these four types and how you can implement them into your questioning strategy.

Part III:
Five Levels of
Questioning Strategy

When we look at the art of questioning we need to understand that there are different *types* of questions, but there are different *levels* of questioning. In general, most people tend to use a very narrow questioning level. As professionals we need to widen and be able to use questions effectively on all levels.

Basic and narrow focused closed questions. This forum focuses on soliciting basic answers, many of which can be answered with *yes, no* or some other simple response. This type of questioning is useful if all you need is a simple response or piece of information.
- What is your name?
- What is your phone number?
- What is your position?

Basic and narrow focused open questions. This forum takes the closed question to a different level, but is still focuses on a specific product or piece of information. More information is provided but the projected response is still very basic.
- How do you say your name?
- How does your phone number go?
- How would this feature work for you?

Product or situation focused open questions. This involves a broader scope of information that is still situation-specific or product-oriented. We are probably still using the same terms as the previous question forums. Although this method gives us more information about the specific item, the big picture remains somewhat limited.

- Tell me about your name?
- How is it you came to live where you do?
- Give me an overview of your current office equipment operations?
- What do you have now as far as banking services?

Goal, visionary and future oriented open questions.
This forum takes us away from specific situations or product and into an even broader arena of information. We take in a more expansive picture of the person and their situation, and gain some insight into motives. We have probably dropped the words associated with a product or situation that had been used in the previous three levels.

- In your opinion, how important is a name?
- If you could change anything about your office operations, what would it be?
- When thinking of your financial picture, what priorities come to the top?

Value and motivational oriented open questions: With this forum we expand even further into the person's view of the world, business and life. We also get a more refined idea as to their motivations and values.

- What is it that got you started in business?
- If you were to start over, what would you do differently? Why?
- What are your main objectives and why did you choose them?
- What makes it so important to accomplish these changes in your office operations?

The graphic of concentric circles on the next page offers a visual of these levels of questioning. Each type and level gets larger and broader as the type and amount of information that the question draws out widens. As we move out we also tend to draw out more motivational and value-based information as well. Our focus is not on a product or specific situation, but on the views and feelings of the person with whom we are communicating.

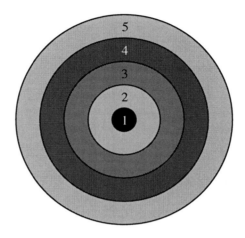

5. Value and motivational oriented open questions

4. Goal, visionary and future oriented open questions

3. Product or situation focused open questions

2. Basic and narrow focused open questions

1. Basic and narrow focused closed questions

Take a moment to think about the questions you currently use, and decide where they would fall within the above graphic.

VALUES, MOTIVES AND DECISIONS

"No man has a good enough memory to be a successful liar." – Abraham Lincoln

All people have values, motives and decision processes that they use every day. Most people, however, do not really understand or are unable to articulate their core values, motives and decision processes.

Consider and list your own values and motives and define on what you base most of your decisions. The more self-aware you are of these things, the more you'll be able to tune into the values, motives and decisions of others.

The following definitions might help.

Values are those ideals our conscience uses to tell us what is right or wrong. Let's agree that we value family time as very important. We've just been given a choice between going fishing (you decide what you want to put in place of fishing), or going to a family member event.

Most of us will sense a degree of stress in picking between the two options. We enjoy the fishing and place a high value on our personal time and independence, but still want to fulfill the value of family time. Which one will win out?

Typically the value that is stronger is the value that usually wins. If we choose the lesser of the two values, we may feel guilty or cheated.

The same is true of our customers when buying.

A customer has a value of self-preservation and keeping their career on track. They also have a value of consistency and not continually changing their mind and breaking promises. Your sales proposal puts them in a dilemma in which they can make themselves look really good and assist their career, but it also requires them to compromise some promises and commitments they had previously made.

Which value will win out?

Will their choice today create a problem for them or your relationship in the future?

This is why understanding a person's values are so important. If we can help the customer fulfill both values we have a sale and a strong relationship. If we cannot and the customer chooses self-preservation over consistency, they may create internal problems for themselves or be seen as selfish and not a team player, which could in turn hurt their career path.

If they choose consistency they could miss a great opportunity for their company and the team's productivity and profit. Part of the salesperson's job is to help the customer find a solution that addresses their key values.

When the term "buyer's remorse" comes up, many times it is a conflict of values that causes the return. Yet if we think about our communications with customers and people in our lives, do we understand any of their values? Might this be why some people will not buy from us or we have challenges in a relationship?

If we do not understand the key values, we may be violating them without knowing it; thus, a poor connection with that person.

Values control actions. Suppose a group of people come across a serious auto accident. People are trapped inside, gasoline is spilling all over the place, sparks are flying and people are calling for help.

Without hesitation a couple of people dive into the fray and try to save those who are trapped, almost oblivious of the danger to them. Others stand back and are torn between getting involved and running away. All the people have a value of self-preservation, but what happened to the people rushing into help?

Did their value of a life override their self-preservation? The answer is probably *yes*.

Meanwhile the bystanders go home and feel guilty, especially if someone died and they might have made the difference. Their value of self-preservation was the strongest.

Now let's take a psychopathic individual who really has no values, does not see life as having value and kills for the thrill of it. It is very difficult for most of us to understand how anyone could not have that value to some degree, but assuming everyone has the same values as we do is not reality. The psychopath's value of self-gratification is much stronger than any life value.

Values influence our actions and decisions everyday whether we realize it or not. The more we understand our own values and the values of others, the more effectively we can address those values or avoid violating them.

Here is a short list of some *values* people may have:

Self-preservation	*Family*	*Value of a life*
Consistence	*Honesty*	*Commitment*
Value of my word	*Love*	*Self-gratification*
Power over others	*Revenge*	*Self-promotion*

Competitiveness	Sense of game	Creativity
Value of change	Traditions	Human value
Conformity	Results Oriented	Control
Parental ability	People growth	Personal growth

Prioritize the above list from your personal view. Now have your spouse or a few friends do the same, and finally, compare. If we assume everyone prioritizes the same as we do, we'll find ourselves missing the sale.

How do we uncover and discover the values of others? We ask questions, the answers to which provide clues to the customer's values.

The majority of people will not simply state their values, perhaps because they may not know them, but also because it is not how our society communicates.

Laying out all your values, motives and self-perception is very risky at the least, but most people hearing it would feel very uncomfortable. So we must listen for clues to those values.

At that point the challenge becomes what kind of questions help us to bring out these values? Well, all information from others can be a clue but there are questions that can be formulated to bring out more of these clues.

Let's start with something simple. You would like to see a movie tonight but know that your partner likes to stay home.

You could ask:

> *"Do you want to see a movie tonight?"* and take a chance at getting a "No." (2nd level question)

An alternative way might be to ask:

"Remember that last show we saw that you liked so much? What was that movie you liked about again?" (5th level question)

The answer might be something along these lines:

"Oh the action was great. It really entertained me."

To which you might respond:

"Well, how would you feel about experience that again this evening?" (5th level question)

You will probably have a greater chance of a "Yes" with the second question because you uncovered a value (self-gratification) and resold a result based on that value.

Do you normally communicate this way? How might the responses of those in your lives change if you did?

Now let's take a sales interview with a company president:

"Mr. President, what was it that has driven you to build the company to this level of performance?" (5th level question)

"Well I have always been competitive and enjoy a daily dose of competition in different forms, so I guess I always found a way to make a competition out of just about everything."

"I have met many competitive people, not all are as successful as you. What kind of obstacles does your competitiveness create?" (5th level question)

"Well one is that not all people function the same way in a competitive environment. I have had to

really pick the right people that can function under the pressure and turn it into energy."

"What is it that you looked for in these people that told you they could be a good fit?" (5th level question)

"One of the most important is a sense of self-confidence to take on new ideas and challenges. I also look for creativity and a sense of independence from them. At the same time they need to be people-oriented so we can build a strong team."

"Why is creativity and independence important?" (5th level follow-up)

"Well I need people that can continually come up with new and different approaches to our market and product. The independence gives me people that will take action and put things into motion very quickly. On occasion I spend a lot of time pulling the reins in, but that is better than having to constantly be trying to motivate a group."

"That is interesting, if you had to pick the one strength that is the most important in your people, what would it be?"(5th level question)

"Hmmm. That I believe would be the people skills. I pick that because most people can not get a strong team performance going without it. Without a team it gets really tough to get things done."

We have asked five questions of this executive, all of which were in the 4th and 5th level. What would you say are some of his values? Note that each question was developed from the previous answer. That means we had to listen.

From his answers we might conclude that he is competitive, has a sense of game, is creative, values quality people and is long-range-oriented and willing to give away some of his power for a better result. He is not a control freak, does not look for details and is not conformity driven.

So how would we package our proposal to him? It would have to be long- range-oriented with results as a key. It would also have to respect the value of his people and deal with their development as a team to enhance their competitiveness. I would avoid soft fuzzy stuff; no talk about control or conformity, and avoid making him the king.

How often do you work with customers in this manner? If you did, how might it change the results? Can you confidently tell me what the values are of each of your major customers?

This concept may be very foreign to you, but believe us when we say it can make selling a very fun and exciting process where everyone wins for the right reasons.

"Ninety percent of our assets are standing in our own shoes!" - Unknown

Motives and values can many times cross, looking and feeling the same, but motives may come from our base values.

Let's assume someone values consistency, which means doing the same quality of performance every time. This may cause a motive for action to be "people pleasing" because they want to appear to be very dependable to others.

Motivation is a motive; a reason for doing something with "tion" attached puts it into action. Most motives are emotion-based and backed or rationalized with logic.

One classic example is the 50-year-old married man buying an expensive sports car so he can feel 22 again, and then having to figure out how to logically justify this purchase to his conservative wife.

Many motivators are driven by fear or gain. I may have a fear of loss of some type and am motivated to avoid that loss. If the motivation or emotion is strong enough, it could override my values.

If one of my core values is honesty but I am put in a position in which everything that is important to me could be lost, I may end up lying to prevent the loss. My motivation -- fear of loss -- is stronger than my value of honesty at that time.

Many salespeople assume everyone has the same motivators. Some, for example, will focus on pricing with every customer. They are most likely assuming the buyer's motivation is getting the best deal, which means price not value. As such, they focus their exchanges with the customer on product and price, rather than taking value and motivation into consideration.

The salesperson who takes time to understand their customer's values and motives will package the product around them. Almost always, the latter salesperson ends up with a larger margin of sale for the same product to the same customer.

Consider this brief list of possible motives:

Fear of loss	Possible gain	Feeling important
Feeling of Belonging	Survival	Security
Being loved	Doing the right thing	How I am viewed
Ego	Self-Promotion	Recognition
Love of family	Immediate gratification	Self-actualization

Prioritize the above list from your personal view and then have your spouse or a friend(s) do the same. Now compare. If we assume everyone prioritizes the same as we do, we'll find ourselves missing the sale.

Whether we are in sales, management or serving in a parenting role, understanding other people's motives can help us change their behavior and decisions. When we understand what it is that moves them to action, we can present the solution in those terms and get a very different result.

Let's look at how we can use our level 4 and 5 questions to uncover possible motives in our customers. Our scenario is an office equipment salesperson talking to a mid-level operations manager about new equipment.

"Ms. Manager, could you give me a brief overview of your operations here?" (3rd level question)

"Sure. We handle all the documentation for the other departments. This includes all legal documents, correspondence, manuals and other key paper work.

Our job is to make sure everything is done correctly, including proof-reading, formatting, printing, binding and delivering the product.

We have 25 people on staff with a variety of backgrounds and disciplines. We have a variety of processing and printing machines, both old and new."

"Sounds like a big job with some important responsibilities. How is your performance measured?" (3rd level question)

"Well, accuracy is one of the biggest, especially on the legal side. The next would be speed of delivery. We're often given short deadlines because we are the last to receive projects, and other departments don't

seem to understand the amount of time needed to complete the task. "

"Everyone seems to have key issues that create frustrations. What might these be for you?" (5th level question)

"Hmm. Well, the time pressure oftentimes puts my people on edge and morale drops. This is heightened when our equipment fails to function and adds to the workload. Many times we end up with overtime because of the equipment, and then our costs go up."

"So how does all of this reflect on you and how your supervisor views your performance?" (5th level question)

"The boss understands the issues we face, but he has to be accountable for cost and performance also. We both agree I spend too much time putting out fires instead of improving the operation. So I would like to gain some control over the issues so the department can get better production without overworking the staff."

"So what would be your major objectives in addressing the situation?" (4th level question)

"I think eliminating the equipment problems would be number one, then looking at how to make the operations more efficient for my staff, which would go a long way on improving morale. If those two things happened I probably would have more time to actually manage."

"Let's assume we could make this happen for you. What would be in it for you personally?" (5th level question)

"I would feel better about my performance and how my staff is feeling. It would be nice to have some fun

again instead of all the overtime. Maybe we could even get some time off."

"I'm curious, how would you spend your time off?" (5th level question)

"I'd probably spend more time with my kids and family. It seems we never have enough time together. I had to miss a school program last week because of a deadline."

"So if we could reduce your equipment problems as well as improve the effectiveness of the staff, thereby reducing the departments stress level and freeing up some of your time, how would you see us doing business?" (*Conceptual close*)

As we examine the questions and the answers, do we discover clues to both values and motives for this manager?

Values might include people, consistency and quality of life. Motivations are survival, how he is viewed by others, love of family and loss of quality of life. Do you see any others? Note that each question flows from the answer preceding it.

If we can tie our solution to these issues, we have a much better chance of making a sale and creating a long-term relationship with this customer.

As you went through the responses, were you tempted to jump in with a product or solution instead of more questions?

Were you tempted to alter the direction of the questions and be more focused on product?

The challenge is to stay focused on values and motives first; the product will come in when needed.

Also, put yourself in the manager's place. As you give these responses, what happens to the picture in your mind?

- Does helping our customers create an image of their situation make it more real?
- Does this image bring out the values and motives for the customer?
- Does this help make the customer more receptive to a solution?
- Does it help move the customer forward to a decision faster?

Isn't it interesting how easily we can be drawn into selling product instead of uncovering values and motives?

Look again at the example, and notice how no product was introduced or discussed, yet at the end we asked for a commitment to go forward. We call this the *"Conceptual close,"* which means the customer has bought the *concept*. Now we just have to show how we can actually perform and close the order.

Can you see yourself applying this strategy?

Decisions are not always made in the same way or on the same basis. Much of this has to do with personality types, background, values and motivations.

Generally speaking, we know men and women are different in many ways, including how information is processed and decisions are made. Men often look at *how*, the mechanics and solutions. Women tend to look at *why*, the emotional side of it, and feel the need to talk it out.

We use a method called DISC to explore personality styles by separating them into four distinct groups. Most people possess characteristics of all four styles, but generally one of the four is dominate in their decision-making.

The types are:

Dominance/Pragmatic: These people tend to be very straight-forward and results-oriented. They want to know what a product will do, not how it will do it. They are not very detail-oriented but they do seem to be driven and can come across very strong. They have a tendency to make very quick decisions based on very little information. They utilize more logic than emotion in their decisions.

Common Positions: executives, entrepreneurs, some politicians, salespeople

Influencer/Extrovert: This group includes the people-people. They love to talk and interact and need to be around others. They are not detail-oriented and find it difficult to stay on task. They may come across as flighty, and will need hand-holding to make decisions. They employ more emotion than logic in their decisions.

Common Positions: politicians, salespeople, performers

Steadiness/Supportive: These folks are driven by cooperation. They want everyone to get along, and service is a very core value. It takes time to build their trust. They will say *we* before *I*. They need a lot of information and trust before they will make a decision, and will generally look for a consensus from others. They use more emotion than logic in their decisions.

Common Positions: supervisors, managers, teachers, nurses, social workers

Competent/Compliant: These are very detail-oriented people. They want to know how something works rather than what it will do, and they require a lot of tangible proof. They also require hand-holding in decision-making and a lot of time. More logic than emotion plays into their decisions.

Common Positions: engineers, accountants, research scientists

Again, all of us have characteristics of all four groups, but which dominates in our decision-making?

As we listen to and observe our customers, we need to determine their dominant type and modify our approach to match.

Want more on the DISC behavior profiles? Check out the information on the website
www.thesellinggap.com/products.html.
Indicate you have "The Selling Gap" book and get a FREE profile consultation!

Another issue is time orientation. This refers to the time period we reference when making decisions. We break this into three time periods:

Past-oriented: Decisions and choices are based on the past and past experiences. A good example is an older person who went through the Great Depression of the 1930s. They are very conservative and often have a great fear of loss. They tend to save everything and their choices frequently reflect their past experiences. Even very young people can be past-oriented.

Present oriented: Decisions are based on what will happen now: can I get it now, what will it do for me now? They are not concerned about yesterday or tomorrow, only today. Their view is very short term.

Future-oriented: Decisions are based on what the results will be down the road. These people look at future results: what the future value will be and whether they are willing to give up something today for future benefits.

It's easy to see the complications people can present to us as salespeople. With values, motives and decision-making thrown together, infinite possibilities abound.

Let's look as a few possible combinations and how we might work with them.

1. An executive/owner with a dominate style with future orientation; values include results and integrity motivated by ego and importance.

We would want to be very direct, avoid small talk, discuss future objectives and talk in terms of future results and how it will make the client look.

2. An executive/owner with a dominate style with present orientation; values are honesty and value of people motivated by how he is perceived by others.

We would want to be very direct and talk about today's situation and what can happen now, with an, emphasis on how his employees will benefit and see him as a good leader.

3. A small business owner with an influencer style who is future oriented with values of quality of life and family, and motivations of belonging to the community.

We have to take control of the conversation, use shorter and less open questions, keep him on track, and discuss his future with his business and community and how your solution will affect his quality of life.

4. An engineer on a construction project has a competent style and is past- oriented with values of

consistency and conservation, and motivations of wanting everything to be in order.

Patience and more patience will be required. Be certain of all the facts he needs and provide them on time. Talk about avoiding loss and how everything will be in order and on time. And demonstrate how you will not have mistakes.

To help uncover values, motives and decision processes, use level 4-5 questions that ask people to choose or compare between one idea or the other and why. This can quickly help isolate the information for you.

"If you had to choose between developing your team or generating more profits, which would it be and why?" (5th level question)

"Let's suppose you could only pick one of the solutions we have discussed. Which would it be and why?" (5th level question)

This is a very dynamic process and can change on a daily, if not minute by minute, basis. The key is to focus on how the customer sees their situation, how they view themselves and what is important to them. Once that has been revealed, we have a much greater opportunity for a sale and long-term relationship with them.

By the way, where is your product in all of this?

"To get others to come into our ways of thinking, we must go over to theirs, and it is necessary to follow in order to lead." – William Hazlitt

Listening skills:

We have mentioned several times that we have two eyes, two ears and one mouth and need to use them in that ratio of 4:1. So how do we improve our listening and observing abilities?

Over the years I've developed many trainers. There were also many that I would not approve for certification. One of the first points I make with new trainers is that they need to drop their egos at the door when they do training. Their first duty is to focus on the people they are training. Those who could not leave their ego at the door or truly listen were quickly eliminated. The same is true of us as salespeople. Our focus needs to be on the customer, not on us.

Our mind has to be focused on what is being said, and not just the words but the meaning behind the words. If you ask someone, *"How you doing?"* and you get a half-hearted response, what might the words really be saying?

- Might the tone of voice, facial expression and physical stance be saying something different than the words?
- Could we read that it is not ok?
- Could it be a very bad day?
- Could it be a very tired person?
- Could there be a very serious issue they need to talk about?

People oftentimes overlook this element and miss the verbal and physical cues. Poor communications and a missed sale often result. Think of the times you have given a response and yet felt very different from the words you used. What would have happened if someone had picked up on it and pursued it? What if someone had simply ignored it?

- The art of listening starts with us shutting up our external vocal orifice and shutting off our internal ego voice.
- It is only when we are quiet both externally and internally that we can truly begin to really listen.

- Internally we need to shut off the worry and concern over how we are doing or how others may perceive us.
- With this internal noise shut down we can now fully concentrate on the feelings and meanings being transmitted. At this point, the brain opens itself to broader thinking and possibilities.
- This means we also shut off the external world. We stop what we are doing, look the person in the eye and posture ourselves so we can view the person's body language. Doing things such as taking notes and mirroring the other person's body language helps us to stay focused on listening.

Here is the LADDER acronym to help us remember:

Look at the person
Ask questions
Defer judgment
Drop defenses
Empathize with them, which means understand, not agree
Reflect on the information, including an occasional pause

Once you have done the LADDER, you can respond to the person on their level and to their needs.

An executive I know said, "Learn to breathe through your nose. It keeps your mouth shut!"

Follow-up questions:

In working with the questioning skills and the **5 Levels of Questioning,** I find many people ask the open questions but can get stuck on the second or third question and staying in control of the interview.

Here is where having follow-up questions can pull you through. These are very short, open questions that simply keep the customer talking and providing you even more information. We call these the Million Dollar Questions.

Why do we need to ask a second, third or even fourth question? Psychologists have shown that it may take two to four additional questions before people will provide their "true" answer or feelings.

So always probe until you see a body language change. This indicates a "true" or "feeling" answer is coming. Yes, this will take you out of your comfort zone as well as your customer's, yet it is at this point at which the real power of persuasion comes into play.

Here are some examples of *follow-up questions*:

"Tell me more about that."

"Why is that?"

"How did that happen?"

"What did you do?"

"What resulted?"

"Oh?"

"How is that?"

You will note these are not complicated questions. Anytime you want the customer to tell you more or go deeper into a subject, use a very simple *follow-up question*. If you have a young child at home, you might be able to learn from them and their continual asking.

Mastering the 5 Levels of Questioning Summary:

1. We must understand people's values.
2. Values and motivators affect decisions.

3. Conflicting values must be addressed to avoid future problems.
4. Character types make decisions differently.
5. Time orientation affects decisions.
6. The 5 levels of questioning can uncover values/motives/decisions.
7. Listening effectively requires both external and internal quiet.
8. Use follow-up questions to keep the customer talking.

Section 5: Recommendation And Agreement

Part I:
Conceptual Agreement
Strategy

"I signed two new advertisers to annual contracts last week and have three prospect appointments scheduled for this week. The magic question was, "What is your vision for your business?" Then I tailored my recommendation around their answer. And the conceptual close was SO AWESOME!!!!! I got chills as I was asking it, in anticipation for their collective, undisputable agreement that we should do business!! It was such a rush. Thanks for your guidance, Harlan. Much appreciated..." – Lori Thompson, advertising/ corporate sales trainer

It's amazing how one idea that works can completely change our perspective on what we do. Even an experienced sales trainer can get results from a new and different strategy. For those of you challenged by asking for the order, try this strategy and see what happens:

Conceptual Agreement: If we have the customer seeing the solution, feeling the solution, we can now "close" on the "concept" even before we bring our product in. If the customer "buys" the "concept," then the *Recommendation Step* simply backs up the "concept" and completes the sale. We use *Trial Questions* to get the *Conceptual Agreement*.

> *"You have painted an interesting picture Mr. Jones. If we could address this to your satisfaction, do we have your business?"*

> *"We have discussed several issues, Mr. Jones. If we could get the results you wanted within your timeframe, are you prepared to commit the people and time needed to make it happen?"*

> *"Mr. Jones, obviously there are several issues here that will cost you a considerable amount of time and money. Suppose we could cut that time and cost by 20 to 30 percent. Would that be worth an investment of $000.00 to accomplish your objectives?"*

Yes, we are asking for the order at this time. If we have the customer's agreement and it is strong enough, we may not even need to bring in our product.

It's important to reiterate that the customer buys the "results" of your product rather than the product itself. If we have them emotionally involved with a clear picture of their situation, do they really need all the details?

Or are they simply grateful they have a possible solution and trust you because of how you clarified their problem?

It is critical to understand this, because every day thousands of salespeople get their customers to this point and blow it by dumping their product on the buyer. Don't fall into this common trap. This is when the customer often pops up with objections from left field and goes on to buy from the next salesperson offering a similar solution. To avoid this you need to create a *Trial Question* or series of *Trial Questions* you can use to get a *Conceptual Agreement*.

By asking these *Trial Questions* at this time and throughout the *Discovery Step*, it is possible to get a very good feel for the customer's willingness to buy. It can also help us to narrow down exactly what needs to be presented in our *Recommendation Step*. If we can obtain a commitment to take action at this time, then we simply need to provide only enough information to help the customer justify going ahead. Our product now becomes a tool to address the customer's issue, rather than the product itself being the issue.

Attempting to secure a *Conceptual Agreement* also can help us know whether we are on the right track with the right person. It can indicate whether we are moving too fast and need to back up or are wasting our time and need to move on for better opportunities.

Once we've received a clear picture of the customer's situation and they have the same picture, we can move on to the *Recommendation Step* if needed.

Part II:
Recommendation
Strategies

"It is impossible to make a good deal with bad people."
Zig Ziglar, motivational sales speaker

"I have a question for you, Don," says Bill, a customer. "Why don't you give us all the facts and benefits on this equipment like the other competitors do?"

"Well Bill," Don replies, "the truth is you probably know more about this piece of equipment and all its stats than I do. My question is what do you want to buy: a piece of equipment for your yard, or an ongoing result with a payback for you?"

"That's why I buy from you, Don. You think like I do," Bill says.

This was an actual conversation between a top-selling equipment salesman and one of his newer customers. Our next step is another "bridge" to bring us smoothly into our recommendation and tie our *Engagement, Discovery* and *Recommendation* together.

Within this next step are some key concepts to keep in mind:

1. **Have we based our recommendation on our own ideas or those that have come from the customer's input in the Discovery Step?** The Recommendation should **always** be based on the customer's input.

2. **Have we been specific enough?** We must be very specific in our recommendation. Instead of being vague, we should be prepared to suggest a particular model, make, concept, program or item we feel will meet the needs uncovered together by ourselves and the customer. Too many options create "brain lock" and no decision. In fact, many different tests have shown that when more options are given to people, fewer decisions are made and a greater percentage of people make no decision at all.

3. **Have we tied the emotional aspect of the customer into our recommendation bridge statement?** If we have completed the *Discovery Step* and *Conceptual Agreement* on the *Customer's Issues*, then the *Recommendation Step* simply fills in the blanks for the customer.

"Mr. Jones, based on what you have told me, I see that a customized teambuilding program will provide the results needed to keep the organization on target and productive to meet and exceed your personal objectives. Here is how we can accomplish this."

What did we recommend?   Customized team-building.

What will it provide?   The meeting of on-target, productive and personal objectives -- the very issues the customers brought forth in the *Discovery Step*.

In other words, we have summarized the main issues Mr. Jones revealed in the *Discovery Step* and incorporated them into our *Recommendation Step.*

To fully grasp the *Recommendation Step,* we need to go to our car, unlock the trunk and bring in our product or service that has been recommended. And then what? Do we pull out all our literature and brochures and talk about every fact and feature there is?

Hopefully you're saying, *"No!"*

We need only to provide information that is needed for Mr. Jones to complete his positive decision. If the fact or feature does not fit or address something brought out in the *Discovery,* then it is not needed here.

So we want only the "key" facts or features that will clearly tie into the customer's wants and desires.

We also want to provide an "emotional" tie to these facts and features that reverts to those "emotional factors" uncovered in *Discovery.* What we present to Mr. Jones would look like this:

> "First, Mr. Jones, this program will provide skill-building and behavior changes in the organization. *This is done thorough minimal lecture and a major emphasis on direct coaching and participation.* This means immediate application and thus productivity gains almost immediately. And productivity is what you're after, isn't it?"

> "The skills and behavior changes will be reinforced by space sessions over time. *This has been proven to very measurably increase the retention and continued development of the skills and behaviors.* This will translate into a quicker cohesion of the merged groups and increase their productivity much faster. Now time is money in this case isn't it? (Use a piece of evidence.) By the way, here is a white paper

on another firm that had similar issues and the results this program provided. .... Is this the type of results you need?"

"With the customized program, material will be tailored to your organization's needs and objectives. *This means a quicker acceptance of your organizational goals and procedures.* With quicker acceptance along with skills and behaviors, you'll meet if not beat your timeline goals. Now that will not only make you feel good, but look good, won't it?"

Let's take these fact/benefit/result statements apart.

We start with a fact or feature of your product, such as (above) skill and behavior change, material tailoring and skill building. A fact is anything that can be proven by an outside source or third party.

We follow it up with a benefit of the fact or how the fact/feature may work. The third part is taking the "key results" information and emotion from the *Discover*, and tying it to the benefit using the customer's language. Finally, we ask a verification question which rephrases the "key results" emotion or outcome (not the product) and confirms that it's what the customer wants.

When providing your fact/feature – benefit/process – results/emotion – clarifying question, we need to be very specific: use only one fact/feature with one benefit/process with one results/emotion. If we were to give multiple facts or benefits it becomes very confusing communication. When confused, do you buy?

If you have *Reverse Engineered* your product, you already have laid out all the facts/features and results. You simply need to pick which fit best and use them.

Part III:
Trial Questions

I have watched with amazement the setting in motion of these concepts. Morris, a highly experienced salesman, is one person I've observed up close. As we sat side by side making cold calls, I observed how he transitioned into his *Discovery Strategy*, which consisted primarily of only *Trial Questions*. Soon thereafter he began using the *Conceptual Agreement* and closed the sale with little or no product information.

Trial Questions really do work!

So let's see if we can move into the **Agreement Step** of the process by using *Trial Questions*. *Trial Questions* are opinion-asking, not decision-asking, and are open-ended.

Consider the following *Trial Questions*:

"Now Mr. Jones, how does this fit your picture so far?"

"What items, if any, would need to be addressed before approving this project?"

"Assuming these items were addressed to your satisfaction, would we be moving forward on the approval?"

Please note we do not bring the product into the questions; rather, the results that are desired. After all, isn't that what the customer is buying?

Based on the responses to such questions we can determine if we should continue to go for the *Agreement* or, if the customer is hesitant, consider what other strategy can be implemented.

It is important to note that we are not talking about *objections* at this time even though we may get some. We are simply determining whether or not we need to add the *Motivation Step* or go directly to the *Agreement*.

Part IV:
Motivational Strategies

The *Motivation Step* is designed for the buyer who has said "Yes" most of the way, has qualified, and has clarified the sale will benefit them, yet for some reason still has hesitated to commit.

The best way to view this step is as a summary of the sale to this point. If it has been a long process and a great deal of information has been passed, the buyer may have been disengaged from the emotional aspect of the purchase. It's important to remember that most of the time we buy on emotion and justify with logic. We may need to bring the customer back to the emotional attachment at this point.

We accomplish this by summarizing what the customer wanted and the emotions that were attached to that. When we do this in the form of a "word picture" it can be very powerful and bring them back to the buying point.

Most people see things in picture form in their mind's eye; this is why it is so powerful. As we mentioned earlier, the word *fire* more likely than not evokes a "vision of flames." Most people are visual-oriented and very motivated and influenced by pictures. The picture, however, must be clear, concise and contain only elements from the *Discovery*. If you do this well, you will be projecting the customer into the future using your product and the results of that use.

In his research on resistance, Dr. Eric Knowles shows that choices are far easier to make when people are projected to the future where they already have made the choice and are experiencing the results. Here is an example:

> "Mr. Jones, suppose you went ahead with this program. It is six months from now and the training is completed. Your managing vice president is going over the numbers and is amazed at the production levels and minimal turnover you have achieved with the new merged group. He indicates you're showing strong leadership and doing far better than most. It is a definite feather in your cap. Now isn't that the picture we have been talking about? When was the start date for the first session again?"

A very quick summary in the form of a word picture can have dramatic results when done effectively with true sincerity and enthusiasm. Be sure to use a *Trial Question* and do not be afraid to go for the *Agreement*.

At times a customer may be motivated and need the product but still hesitates, and it might be difficult to isolate the reason. We can pull out some old but proven tools to get us to the *Agreement*.

Let's go to Ben Franklin and his decision-making columns (the Church Hill Close for our friends from the United Kingdom) or use the old Doug Edwards summary close. These are designed to take the fence-sitter and move them through the decision process.

If you read *Poor Richard's Almanac* you will find the Ben Franklin decision process. The tool is used in this way:

> "Mr. Jones, I realize this may be a challenging decision for you. You of course know about Ben Franklin and how he is known for his common sense approach. Let's do what old Ben did when he had decisions to make.

Ben would take a piece of paper and make two columns. One is marked for and the other against. Let's do that. Ben then would list all the reasons for going ahead with the decision. So let's list them. (Have the customer do the writing and you help him with all the pros.)

Okay, now let's list all the against. (At this point you refrain from comment and let them do it alone.) Okay, now Ben would simply count up the items in each column and the column with the largest total was what he did. Let's count them up. It's obvious isn't it, Mr. Jones? Did you want to do the program in one group or two?"

It's important to take this process seriously. It does work when approached correctly and has been used by many of the most successful salespeople, even over the phone.

The Summary Close is designed to get the fence-sitter or the one that simply will not tell you what is holding them back. It is effective but needs be planned or at least worked on in practice sessions. Here is how it goes:

"Mr. Jones, I am sensing some hesitation on your part about going ahead with this. Would you mind telling me what it is?"

(Do not stop for an answer.) Is it...(Here you verbally list all the possible reasons for hesitation such as the company, our delivery, the color, the size, our president, the timing, the coordination needed, the length of time, and so forth.

Always leave cost and other common major issues until the end.

When you get down the list and they say, "Yes, that's it," you go into *Objection Response* and then to the *Agreement*.

Once more, you need to know your product and customer to make this tool work. All three of these, the word picture, Ben Franklin Decision and Summary Close, can be used when needed, but are not needed every time. Therefore they need to be practiced repeatedly to work efficiently.

Another point about these strategies is they cause the "resistance" to be brought out and put on the table. This fits with Dr. Knowles' Omega Strategies on acknowledging the resistance to take it down or remove it.

If your *Discovery Strategy* is effective, you will rarely need these tools.

Get Dr. Knowles "Omega Strategies" on DVD at
www.thesellinggap.com/products.html.
Indicate you have "The Selling Gap" book and receive
two FREE CD's on persuasion!

Part V:
Agreement Strategies

Now that we have the customer saying "yes" and indicating a forward motion with their answers to our *Trial Questions*, we need to get the *Agreement*.

The *Agreement* can be many things, not just a firm order. Some sales require additional services or information before a final agreement. Items such as engineering, legal, government approvals, logistic issues, etc., may need to be finalized before a purchase is finalized.

At this point, we do need confirmation to firm up what has been accomplished so far. We need some kind of assurance that the customer will go forward provided the remaining issues are completed as needed. We also need to be aware of a possible "put off" objection, which we'll discuss in depth in a later chapter.

How should we request the order and secure the *Agreement*? Several simple tools can help us move in the right direction. It's important to keep in mind that the *Agreement* should be a logical and smooth conclusion to an effective sales call, not some mystical separate action.

The *"Minor Point"* question can be very effective here. *"What was the name to be?"* or *"What delivery date is needed?"* or *"Your purchase order number is?"* We need answers to these questions to complete the order. Simply begin asking them and continue until the customer stops you.

We might also employ the *"Multiple Choice"* question, a modification of the above. *"Did you want the red or the white?"* or *"Will this be cash or check?"* or *"Did you want to run one or two sessions?"* Again, we need this information. We are encouraging the customer to make these small choices and, in doing so, come to a logical conclusion about what we can offer them.

Doug Edwards, one of my former and favorite trainers, sometimes modifies this in an interesting and effective way by using *two* multiple choice inquiries. The first prompts a major decision; the second, a minor one: *"Did you want to do the annual lease or go for the full purchase? By the way, did you want to use your pen or mine?"* When the customer chooses a pen, a minor choice, it carries the major choice.

Elmer Wheeler, another old-timer, sold thousands of eggs back in the day of the malt shop employing another variation if this. A customer who wanted a malt would be asked; *"Do you want one egg or two in your malt?"* Those who usually did not have an egg said, "One." Sales of eggs went though the roof because the question made it seem as if eggs were not optional.

Another form of this is the *"Next Step"* question, which might look something like this: *"This proposal seems to meet your productivity need. What is our next step?"* The customer can now mention whether engineering, logistics or some other element will be needed. Their answer might prompt a call for a purchase order number. The *"Next Step"* question encourages the customer to address any issues that remain.

You might be wondering, "Is this all?" Yes, that's really all there is to it. I use these types of questions on all sales calls. A combination of *Trial* and *Agreement questions* will get you the order. So much for the great mystery of closing!

This should give you a general idea of the sales process and its steps. If followed on a consistent basis, this process will provide you with consistent results. If you use shortcuts or skip steps, however, the results will be less fruitful.

And always remember that once the closing question is asked, SHUT UP AND LISTEN! He who speaks first loses.

The Five Steps Reviewed:

1. The Attention Getting Step
Value or Problem Statement
Problem or Results Oriented Question
Credibility Statement

2. The Discovery Step
Current Situation
Future View
Hurdles
Rewards
>Results
>Criteria
>Emotional Buttons
Conceptual Close of Sale

3. Recommendation Step
Facts/Features
Benefits/Results
Key Factors
Emotional Tie In
Trial Questions

4. Motivation Step
Word Picture
Ben Franklin Close
Summary Close

5. Agreement Step
Minor Point
Alternate Choice
Trial Questions
Next Step

Section 6: Resistance And Objections

Part I:
Six-Step Strategy for Objections

"All problems become smaller if you don't dodge them but confront them. Touch a thistle timidly and it pricks you; grasp it boldly and its spines crumble." – William S. Halsey, U.S. Admiral, Pacific, WWII

Wouldn't it be nice if every time we offered someone a new idea they just accepted it? Yet we know that won't happen. Even we are resistant to change. In fact, you may feel resistant to some of the ideas and applications of this book you are reading.

Why is it that people resist that which is good for them? Why do customers resist your ideas and products?

We have to remember that people are motivated more by fear of loss than rewards from gain. Most of our population falls into a category known as "conformists," or people who like to feel comfortable and often don't seek change because it is uncomfortable and their perception is they may lose something.

I often say, "It is easier to put up with the pain of conformity and settle for less than it is to go through the pain of change and get more." How true it is.

We will break down our study into a step process in order to examine this idea of objections and resistance from our customers. Then we can work on how we might apply that process to some common resistance that might emerge in our work.

During the selling process we can experience resistance any time, in any of the steps along the way. So we need to be able to apply the steps of the process at any time. This requires us to stop thinking about our product, the sale or our fears; rather, we need to focus on the customer and what they are really saying.

We need to stop selling and start the communication process by listening to words, body language, emotions and hidden meanings.

Keep in mind that a well-executed *Discovery Step* and *Conceptual Agreement* will eliminate 99 percent of potential objections that might emerge during and after an interview. This is because the customer has a strong mental picture of the results and already has made the choice to go ahead.

As we proceed through this process you will find the *Mastery of Questions* to be quite valuable. You may even want to review that section. After all, and once again, this is more about communication and understanding than pushing your product.

It is also helpful to be mindful of our own attitudes and feelings toward resistance and objections. Do we tend to run and hide, avoiding confrontation at all costs? Do we not make an attempt that might make someone not like us? Do we lack confidence to control the situation, or say, "Great, I got this one!"

"It's not personal, it's business!" - Donald Trump

The *six steps that can help us overcome objections* include:

1. **LISTEN:** Any time we get resistance or objections we need to stop and really listen, not only to what is being said, but also to what is *not* being said. Just because someone says, "It costs too much," doesn't mean the price is the real issue.

   The reality is that most of the time they are really saying something else. We need to pay attention to voice tone, body language and other indicators.

2. **QUESTION FOR CLARIFICATION:** We need to really be intent on understanding, and because of that, we have to ask for clarification, or question a statement, to be sure we fully understand what was meant. This requires us to question any statement and those that follow as often as needed until we get to the customer's real issue.

   A *real issue* is something you can really and fully grasp mentally, and do not view through a fog or cloud. Until the real issue is understood, there is little need to proceed.

   Note: This step is the one most salespeople jump through too quickly. They hear something about the product and assume that's the issue instead of asking another question and probing deeper. Don't skip over this step. Question until you really have the issue!

3. **UNCOVER HIDDEN OBJECTIONS:** Even though a customer says one thing, does it mean it is the only thing? Psychology tells us people will give us statements hoping to distract us or block us from the real issue. If so, how do we uncover these additional or hidden issues? Psychology also indicates it may take two to three or more questions to uncover a true feeling or issue.

4. **EMPATHY:** Once we have the real issues out on the table we can empathize with the customer.

This does not mean we agree. *Never agree with an objection.* It will solidify the resistance in the customer's mind. Rather, we want to communicate that we understand their situation and would like to help. We can express this in a word, a series of words or a full statement. All we are saying is that we have heard and understood them.

5. **RESPOND:** Now we can determine what tools and approach we need to use to address the real issue creating the resistance. We can bring out more information to *educate*, we can provide more *benefits* to sell the idea, or we can use *questions to lead* the customer to a different conclusion.

6. **TRIAL QUESTION:** Now that we have the customer saying *yes* and viewing the issue differently, we need to check and see if we are actually on track. A *Trial Question* or series of *Trail Questions* can lead us to a conclusion (*AGREEMENT*).

"Success is not measured by what a man accomplishes, but by the opposition he has encountered and the courage with which he has maintained the struggle against overwhelming odds."
- Charles A. Lindbergh

To provide an example, let's use, "It costs too much." So, let's say those are the words we have just heard from our customer.

How do we respond?

First, we LISTEN and do not prejudge, make assumptions or get ready to fight with a counter statement. We nod and politely ask, *"That's interesting. What do you mean by it costs too much?"* (QUESTION for CLARIFICATION)

The customer might respond, "Well, I feel that's a lot of money for the product."

We respond politely, *"Would you tell me why you see it that way?* (QUESTION for CLARIFICATION)

Let's say the response is, "I was talking to another supplier and they said their product was at $ each."

We ask politely in response, *"Will you tell me about their offer?"* (QUESTION for CLARIFICATION)

The customer might say, "They can provide the same type of product for $-- and as far as I can see it looks like the same thing."

We say, *"Please tell me, in addition to your pricing concern, is there anything else that would keep you from going ahead with us?"* (UNCOVER HIDDEN OBJECTIONS)

"I guess not."

So we say, politely, *"So if we were able to justify our pricing and show you additional value, would you be willing to go ahead?"* (UNCOVER HIDDEN OBJECTIONS)

"I guess if you can show me a good reason for the difference."(GAINING COMMITMENT)

We might say, *"I appreciate your concern over the price difference; a good buyer always looks for a good value for the dollar. (EMPATHY) When you look at the total package of delivery, stock, delivery time, your warehouse costs, billing and pricing, which is the most important in the bigger picture?"* (RESPOND)(LEADING QUESTION)

"Well, I guess they all are."

And we say, *"So if we can demonstrate a better total value to you in the bigger picture that ultimately costs you less, you would go forward?"* (RESPOND)

"I guess so." (STATEMENT OF COMMITMENT)

And we say, *"Let's take our total package and do a side-by-side comparison and see what their total value is against our total value. Is that fair enough?"* (RESPOND)

"Sure, sounds good to me."

We take them through a comparison process and show how we have a greater value (SELLING).

We then ask politely, *"Now do you feel this will fill your needs better?"* (TRIAL QUESTION)

"I believe so."

"Great," we say, *"When would you like the first order delivered?"* (TRIAL QUESTION)

Please note that we did not argue or fight with the customer, nor did we cut down the competition or talk about reducing or cutting our prices. We changed the issue from price to total value.

Occasionally we will interact with a customer who speaks in a very blunt manner and tries to get rid of us right away. This is called *up-front resistance.*

It might start with a potential new customer saying, "I am not interested. Go away!" You of course know they have no idea what your service or product is, much less what it could do for them. We obviously have not been able to crack that shell and help them see the value.

We might find this resistance when cold-calling, phone calling or when making drop-in in calls. Often a well-planned **Value or Problem Statement** can address the issue and at least give us the opportunity to deal with the resistance.

A conversation involving a **Value or Problem Statement** might look something like this. Let's initiate the conversation and assume we will always respond in a polite manner:

> *"Mr. Businessman, as a business owner you are most likely looking for ways to increase performance, reduce inputs and save time. Is that correct?"*

> "Yes."

> *"The reason I mention this is our organization has several new ideas to assist companies like yours to reduce input costs and save time, some of them as much as 35 percent. What would a 10- percent input reduction mean to your company?*

> "It sounds interesting, but we have worked with our suppliers to cut all we can so I don't see any reason to invest more time."

> *"That's great. Please tell me what percentage of reduction you have achieved and how?"* (QUESTION for CLARIFICATION)

> "Well, I am not sure of an exact percentage but we have reduced the number of suppliers we are using, and that has saved us time and frustration."

> *"Being in the supply business, we are always looking for new insight into how we might save our customers' input costs without cutting service. What else would you do to reduce your inputs even further?"* (QUESTION for CLARIFICATION...and a change in the base of reference is beginning)

"I am not sure. If we cut more vendors we could lose some bargaining power and services, so we would have to look at cutting the product cost itself."

"So if I understand what you are saying, you have taken several actions to reduce your inputs but have not been able to come up with additional solutions for further savings?" (QUESTION for CLARIFICATION...changes base of reference to "additional solutions" versus "inputs")

"Yes, that would be right."

"Let's assume we have additional ideas and strategies that have worked for others in addressing the very issue you're dealing with. Are you willing to invest 15 minutes to verify how these ideas will work for you?" (Here we use a closed *yes* or *no* to either get moving or get out.)

"Um, I guess we should at least take a look. Could you come back tomorrow at around 10:30 a.m.?" (GAINING COMMITMENT)

"I believe so. Who else should be involved in reviewing these ideas?"

"I would say our main purchasing manager. I can see if he would be available."

"That would be great. Here is my contact information and could I have yours please?"

In this example we only want the opportunity to get the appointment. Notice we never brought out the product but clarified what their issue was and then kept coming back to that issue of reducing inputs.

By getting them talking about it they realized they might be losing something by not listening to us. We also did not use all six steps; only what we needed to get the appointment.

Here is another possible scenario. The customer already uses or has a service. We have gotten their attention in a positive way, but they are just not willing to make a change or do not want to deal with another vendor. Our job is to help them see the value of making a change by helping them see that value.

One way we can do this is by helping them see that they made a good choice before and that they now have the same opportunity to make another good choice.

"Your offer sounds fine, but we have a very solid vendor and see no reason to change."

We LISTEN and do not prejudge, make assumptions or get ready to fight with a counter statement. Instead, we nod and politely ask, *"I appreciate that. Can you tell me what makes them such a solid vendor?"* (QUESTION for CLARIFICATION)

"They helped us get started and have provided us with great service and products."

"Sounds good. If you could change or have anything different about them, what would it be?" (QUESTION for CLARIFICATION)

"Well, they do have a minimum order size that sometimes creates a problem. They also only deliver on certain days which is fine, but it would be nice if we could have special deliveries."

"Other than the current vendor situation, would there be any other reasons that would keep us from doing business?" (UNCOVER HIDDEN OBJECTIONS)

"I really don't know. We are pretty happy with the current supplier."

"So if we could somehow provide a solid reason to give us a try, you would be willing to go ahead with an initial order?" (UNCOVER HIDDEN OBJECTIONS)

"I guess if you could provide a really good reason, we probably would." (GAINING COMMITMENT)

"Obviously you had an opportunity to make a very good choice when you went with your current supplier. Don't you have that same opportunity to make another good choice today?" (RESPOND) (CHANGE THEIR BASE OF REFERANCE)

"Hmm, I guess I hadn't thought of it that way. How do you see it being a good choice?"

"Glad you asked! (EMPATHIZE) *Let's review the value of our total package for you so that good choice can be better understood."* (Review your total proposal and its total value, especially in how it provides value the current supplier does not. Get their agreement as you proceed. (RESPOND) *"Now, do you see the better value for your operation?"* (TRIAL QUESTION)

"I would have to say yes."

"Great. Let's get that initial order set up and program started. What's on your list?" (TRIAL QUESTION)

Please note that, once again, we did not cut down the competition or argue with the customer's choices. We did change their frame of reference from the current vendor to the opportunity to make another good choice.

A similar approach is useful when you are up against a long-term relationship and trying to get a foothold to move forward. Change their base of reference back to when they made the initial choice, not the relationship.

You may be wondering now about all those other objections that come up. Whether they are put-off, prejudicial, unfounded, tests, or just plain unreal, we use the same process to determine what the real issue is. Always remember that until you uncover the real issue it is only a guess at what is really going on in the customer's head.

I have delineated only three categories of objections.

They include:
1. *Real objections,* which are specifically about your product or presentation.
2. *Put-off objections,* which are reactionary, foggy and non-committal.
3. *Prejudicial objections,* or opinions or misinterpretations based on misinformation or a skewed view.

No matter which type you get, use the same process.

Now let's look at step 5: **Responding** to the issue or issues that have been uncovered. Once those issues have been revealed and both the customer and you have a common understanding and picture, you can begin to respond in one of three ways. We use only three ways to keep it simple and easier for the professional to concentrate on the customer.

There are other ways to respond, yet most end up categorized as one of these three methods.

Educate:

Education becomes necessary when information or understanding is lacking. The customer may not be up on the new solutions or technology that's available. They may have some misperceptions or erroneous information helping to create the wrong understanding of the situation or solution.

In order to move forward, we need to put on our teacher hat and help the customer understand the true picture. This may require outside information from experts or sources outside your organization. It may be information that they have not seen or heard.

Be specific in the information you provide and keep it brief. Of course, verify that they understand the information and that it makes sense to them. Don't be like the young preacher who had only one farmer show up for his service.

> *The preacher asked the one farmer what he should do, "Give the sermon or just talk?"*
>
> *The farmer said, "If I go to feed my cows and just one shows up, I still feed 'em."*
>
> *So the preacher lets go and gives his full sermon with all the theatrics and emotion of a truly inspired preacher.*
>
> *When he is done and out of breath, he asks the farmer, "How was it?"*
>
> *The farmer replies, "When only one cow shows up, I don't dump the whole load!"*

An example of this might be introducing a new technology.

When working with an industrial supply company, we often found it necessary to educate people on what the new technology was and how it differed from the old and more common technology. In selling training we often have to help people grasp what is meant by behavioral change and invest time in helping them understand it.

If customers do not understand something, they become uncomfortable. When trust is shaky, no forward motion occurs. *Education helps to eliminate the unfamiliarity.*

This will require you to be prepared with a good understanding of those issues that require education. It also means preparing materials to build credibility and confidence in the information you're providing.

Be sure to verify that the information being provided is indeed making a difference in the customer's knowledge. Use plenty of *Trial Questions* to verify that they understand and see the difference.

Back to Selling (Facts/Features/Benefits):

When we detect the issue about our product or service has not been understood, we need to return to our *Recommendation Step* and use the *facts/features/ benefit/results* that apply to the uncovered issue. If the issue is *not* about our product, do not go back to selling, lest you become the product pusher just like all the other peddlers.

We again need to make sure the *facts/features/ benefits/results* address the uncovered issue and no more. We do not need to relay to the customer everything about the product; just enough to help them justify the product. This may mean we only need to give them one of the *facts/features/benefit/results* or perhaps a dozen to help them feel comfortable.

We still need to verify that the information we provide is actually addressing their issues. So use a lot of *Trial Questions* to verify the *facts/features/benefits/results* have hit their mark.

The *Feel, Felt, Found* Method:

This is an old favorite that works well, but because it is a form of an empathy response, you must ask the QUESTIONS for CLARIFICATION before using *Feel, Felt, Found*. Once we have clarified the real issues and obtained a STATEMENT OF COMMITMENT we can precede as follows:

> *"I appreciate how you Feel about the investment required. Others have Felt the same way until they looked closer at the value and Found that the total package was a real bargain. Let me explain ......* (at this point, transition into educating, selling or leading questions).

The value of the *Feel, Felt, Found* helps get the customer into a different reference and to feel comfortable with the fact that others also have changed their view with this new information. This helps them feel more confident with their decision. It is really an empathy statement.

> *"A wise man changes his mind but a FOOL never will."* – Spanish Proverb

Questions to Lead to a Predetermined Conclusion:

We may find the customer's issue mostly involves an opinion or prejudicial viewpoint. If resistance does not stem from your product or presentation, it is most likely a prejudicial objection. In this case, facts or information rarely can alter the opinion or viewpoint.

Let's suppose your 89-year-old granddad has smoked cigars since he was 18 years old. He enjoys them immensely and feels they are his only remaining pleasure in life. The doctors want him to quit, but you know what his answer will be. This is a prejudicial type issue. All the logic, medical information, common sense and persuasion will have little, if any, effect on the granddad.

How do we deal with these sorts of opinions and prejudicial issues? Let's go back to the section on *"Mastering Questions"* and the Socratic method of questioning. We know where we want the customer to go with their thinking, so by using questions to lead them to a "statement of commitment" we can help create a new position of greater value to them.

We might initiate a dialog with granddad that goes something like this:

> "How do you feel about being around for another ten to twelve years?" (5th level)
>
> *"An old guy like me doesn't want to be around if I'm no good to anyone. No nursing home for me!"*
>
> "I can see it's not fun when the body doesn't work like it use to. What would be important to you to be around for another ten to twelve years?" (creating new issue/5th level)
>
> *"Well, all my friends and most of my family are gone, so I guess it would be the grandkids. Sure would like to see them grow up before I go."*
>
> "Why would that be so important to you, Granddad?"(5th level follow-up)
>
> *"I just like to see people grow. I've always liked the kids, especially the young ones. They are so full of life and nothing bothers them."* (gaining commitment)
>
> "How do you think the grandkids see you, Granddad?" (5th level)
>
> *"I hope they see me as a kind old man who loves 'em. I hope they want to come visit me so I can help 'em out somehow."*
>
> "What I am hearing you say, Granddad is that we need to keep you as healthy and functional as long as we can so you can love your grandkids for as long as

possible. Is that what you are saying?" (Conceptual agreement question)

"Yeah, I guess so." (Gaining commitment)

If you feel uncomfortable with the above conversation, it probably says something about your communications with your friends and family.

As you follow the sequence of questions you'll note how we change and create a new base or important issue for granddad to look from. Now we can talk about his health concerns from the viewpoint of his grandkids versus harping on him about his smoking and how bad it is for him. If this new issue is more important than the cigars, we have a fighting chance.

By leading people to a different base of reference, the idea for change becomes their idea. They make the *"statement of commitment"* (gaining commitment) and now it is hard for them to back off that statement. As in granddad's case, it provides a far more important reference from which to view these issues.

Let's consider now a customer who already has a supplier and the salesperson is their relative. This is a tough one that needs finesse, but again, it can be overcome if you change the customer's base of reference. Getting them off the supplier issue and into "making a good business decision" can make the difference.

Here is how the conversation might go, starting with the customer's response:

"Well, we have been with the XYZ Company for some 15 years now and we've really been very pleased with them."

"Fifteen years? That's a long time! What is it about that relationship that has kept you with them for so long?" (QUESTION for CLARIFICATION)

"They helped my father out when he got started and have always worked with us through the good and bad times."

"Obviously they can't supply everything your business needs. What is different about them compared to your other vendors?" (QUESTION for CLARIFICATION)

"They have great delivery, good pricing, a long line of products and my brother is their salesman."

"Interesting. How long has your brother been with them and how did he get started?" (QUESTION for CLARIFICATION)

"Well my father always wanted us to get some outside experience before coming fulltime into the business, so my younger brother went to work for them about four years ago."

"How long does he plan on staying with them before coming back to the business?" (QUESTION for CLARIFICATION)

"I'm not sure. He seems pretty happy and is doing well, but I am thinking if he's going to return, it will be in a couple more years." (making this a non-issue)

"So when your father started doing business with XYZ, what were the factors that made him choose them at that time?" (QUESTION for CLARIFICATION)

"I think one of the biggest was the smaller order size and some financing help with inventories. Cash was pretty tight then."

"And what have been the issues that have kept you making the same choice?"(changing issue to results)

"Hmm, I would say the complete package of price, delivery, quality and financing."

"In other words, you have made the same good business decision based on the results they provide you and your business?"(changing issue to results)

"Yes, that would be right."(gaining commitment)

"So what I am hearing is that you and your father make good business decisions based on the results a supplier provides you. Would that be right?"

"Yeah, that would be true." (gaining commitment)

"Don't you have the same opportunity now to make a good business decision based on the results we can supply you?"

"Well, I guess we should really take a look."

As long as you know where you want to take the customer, a good questioning sequence can get them thinking about the situation differently. Note that we have several "statements of commitment" as we get them to change their base of reference. We may not be completely over the issue, but now have some real hope of securing some business.

The use of leading-type questioning, or Socratic Method, has been used for generations by all types of successful people in various communications roles. The key is to forget about your product and the sale at that time and focus on the real decision-making issues that could change the outcome.

This takes practice and focus; it evolves from what the customer says and requires a good listener, not just to words but to issues, values and motives as well.

A metaphor that comes to mind is the bullfighter. The bull is ten times the size of the Matador, faster and far more dangerous looking.

The Matador is small, quick on his feet, can think and has a cape. If you ever see a bull fight, the Matador does not move very much at all. The bull does all the work.

The Matador distracts the bull with the cape, maneuvers the bull to where he wants it, wears the bull down and delivers the fatal blow. The idea in responding with the question forum is to be the Matador, not the bull.

Summary:
1. LISTEN
2. QUESTION FOR CLARIFICATION
3. UNCOVER HIDDEN OBJECTIONS
4. EMPATHY
5. RESPOND
    a. Educate
    b. Benefits to sell
    c. Questions to lead
6. TRIAL QUESTION

The following is a piece a trainer once left for me. At 80-some years of age, Lowell had trained thousands of people in how to communicate, manage and sell better. I do not know the author, but it may get you thinking about lowering your prices.

$$$ CUT THE PRICE! $$$
(and your throat)

Considering the cutting of prices in order to outsell the competition?
Forget it!
You can't do it and obtain volume and a better net profit all in one package.

These are the figures presented by a long-deceased publication in an article titled "SIGNIFICANCE OF PRICE CUTTING:"

5% requires 14% more $ volume & handling 20% more merchandise

8% requires 25% more $ volume & handling 36% more merchandise

10% requires 35% more $ volume & handling 50% more merchandise

12% requires 50% more $ volume & handling 74% more merchandise

15% requires 70% more $ volume & handling 100% more merchandise

20% requires 140% more $ volume & handling 200% more merchandise

In brief, if you cut a price 15% on a $100 sale, it is necessary to sell $170 in value. You must handle double the merchandise before you can make a profit of $30 to which the original $100 sale entitles you.

May we suggest you consider these factual figures before you hone the razor?

So think about what it really costs to cut the price just for a sale. If you were the owner and had to pay the bills, would you still cut the price? So do not talk about "cutting the price" or "meeting the price." Instead build value that matches up with the customer's values and motives.

Section 7: Personal Power

Part I:
Self-Perception Strategy

"The Chains of Habit are too weak to be felt until they are too strong to be broken."- Samuel Johnson of Famous Amos Cookies

It is a hot and dusty day with the desert sands blowing about. A stranger traveling to the village notices an old man sitting by a tree with some children. He stops and asks the old man about the village and its people.

"Why do you ask?" queries the old man.

"I am planning to set up my trade business here and was wondering what the people and its culture are like," the traveler says.

"How were they where you come from?" the old man asks.

"They were okay but very cheap and very hard to deal with. Many were not pleasant at all," he answers.

"Well, you'll find people are very much the same in most villages," the old man says, sighing.

Not even an hour later another traveler comes by and stops to talk to the old man.

"Kind sir, could you give me some insight as to the people in the village and what they are like?" asks the second traveler. "My partner in business has asked me to set up shop here if it appears profitable."

"How were they where you come from?" the old man asks.

"Oh, they are wonderful people; I regret leaving and will miss many of them. They were kind and thoughtful people who were loyal to our trade," he says.

"Well, you'll find people are very much the same in most villages," the old man says, smiling.

As the second traveler left, one of the children rebuked the old man as having lied to both travelers.

"My child, I did not lie to either; rather, I told them what was in their heart and mind, for how they see themselves and others is how their world will be!"

The whole idea of higher performance is an interesting science. Countless books have been written on motivation, attitude, goals and success secrets. We have both read a pile of books on the subject and still question if we really understand it.

Which of the two travelers do you think will have more success?

This chapter has been written to help you glean what we feel are the key issues to anyone's success in whatever field they may pursue. You may agree or not agree with the insight we will share, but any books or material on the subject of personal growth and success contains the keys outlined here.

Almost any sales, self-development or self-improvement material available says we need to set goals and review them often.

How many of us have done so and yet not really changed or achieved our objectives? As we see it, one needs to go deeper than just goals. We need to understand ourselves better. What is it that really makes goals work for some and not for others? What is it that drives some to great success and others to average or mediocre results?

The story above indicates, *"As a man thinketh so shall he be,"* and carries a great deal of wisdom. If we are constantly thinking of negative ideas and views we become very negative and cynical. Turn it around and think of only positive and uplifting ideas and we become positive in almost everything we do. All of us know this basic idea and yet we also realize how difficult it can be to maintain on a daily basis. So how do we go deeper and create a foundation that will weather the outside influences that can turn us negative?

Before we deal with goals or attitudes we have to understand our own *self-perception*. By this, do we mean our self-image, our self-confidence or our attitude? Actually, our self-perception provides the foundation for all of these. This is why setting goals and maintaining a positive attitude is not always enough to move us forward. It is our foundation we need to strengthen before other aspects can hold up and support us.

There is a Biblical story that tells about two houses; one built on the sand on the shore and the other built on the solid bedrock. The foundation on the sand is eroded by wind and water. The sand is fluid and moves to its own design. The house built there will surely fail while the house on the bedrock stands up to wind, water and earthquake, all because of its foundation.

Let's examine the idea of *self-perception* as our foundation and see if it makes any sense.

Part II:
Self-Perception Makeup

What is this *Self-Perception*? The word *perception* means:

a. Recognition and interpretation of sensory stimuli based chiefly on memory.
b. The neurological processes by which such recognition and interpretation are affected.
c. Insight, intuition, or knowledge gained by perceiving.
d. The capacity for such insight.

In other words, it is how we see and understand things, and how we value items, experiences and the world around us. It is the ability to understand situations, aspects and the world around us. It is our mind's way of looking at ourselves and our world, both conscious and subconscious.

So what does this all mean to you or me? If we can understand our own *self-perception* and see elements of it that may be holding us back, we can make changes to our foundation. We also can reinforce those aspects that strengthen us.

Here's an example. I recently I had lunch with an old friend I had not seen in years. She had become successful in many ways and had done well for herself and her children, but after 17 years of marriage she also had gone through a very tough divorce. I asked what happened. She said she finally had woken up to some damaging patterns in her marriage; her husband had been verbally abusive and condemning. When it escalated to physical abuse and she found herself slammed against the wall, she knew what she had to do. That night she moved out.

Why would someone get into much less stay in such a situation? Something in her *self-perception* said this is normal, this is what I deserve, this is the way my life is. Even though she was smiling and happy on the outside, on the inside she felt negative thoughts about herself and had created a weak foundation. Once she changed that perception, her life changed, and fast.

With a changed *self-perception* of what was right for her, she went on to pursue a career in sales and was quite successful. When asked about dating and romance, she said she had dated some, but as soon as the negative indicators showed up, she was gone. She knows she is worth more and deserves better and will not settle for less from herself. She sees herself very differently today than she had before. When she changed her self-perception, her whole world changed.

When we change our inward *self-perception* it can dramatically change our outward life. We will change the way we make decisions as well as what we decide. Our actions will also change, and people will notice.

Choice

In a recent presentation about "Frustration and How to Grow From It," I started thinking about choices. We all make choices every time we encounter another human being. Most often we base these choices on our *self-perception*. The way I see it is we make one of two types of choices: a *passive choice* to do little or nothing with the encounter, or an *active choice*, through which we get involved and may take risks based on our *self-perception*.

Let's say you come to the office and Sue, the front desk person, is frowning and in a fowl mood. You note this and say, "Good morning," but get little to no response. You make a passive choice and move on. But what is happening in your mind? *"Sue sure is negative today. She needs to get a life."* This might be the message that is stored and starts building, affecting your image and relationship with Sue. For the balance of the day, every person who comes into contact with Sue may get the same treatment and opinion, workers and customers alike.

Let's go back to the same scene and make a different decision. This time our choice will be an active choice.

First off, we note Sue's mood, say, "Good morning," and get little response. We pause a moment and say to Sue, *"Sue, you seem a bit down this morning. Is there anything I can do to help?"*

She responds, *"Oh, I guess I didn't realize that. I was up all last night with sick kids and didn't get a lick of sleep."*

Now Sue is aware of her mood and both you and she have options as to what comes next. The key point is that your view of Sue is now positive, and she is aware of and can alter her mood.

Zig Ziglar says: "How you see 'em is how you treat 'em!" So when we are engaging with others, if we are continually making passive choices, which are generally motivated by fear or indifference, and then wondering why the relationship is not great, maybe we need to take a more active approach and get involved.

Zig Ziglar, Dale Carnegie, Kevin Hogan and others continually say relationships take work, communication, people skills and risk. They also note that if you have the best interest of the other person in mind, you almost always will say the right thing. Take a chance and make more *active choices* in your life.

"Time is limited, so I better wake up every morning fresh and know that I have just one chance to live this particular day right, and to string my days together into a life of action and purpose. – Lance Armstrong, U.S. cyclist, seven-time winner of the Tour de France, cancer survivor

Self-Perception:

Most people seem to agree that they should be more active in their interactions, especially the more negative or challenging ones. Let's explore what might keep us from being as active as we perhaps should be. In most of my conversations with decision-makers, we talk about what it takes to make a person change their performance. This comes down to three elements, which are:

- Self-perception,
- Self-confidence level and
- Communication skills.

A person can be very strong in one area, but if they are weak in another it will thwart their performance.

If we see ourselves as fully capable and can visualize ourselves in a success position and *truly believe it,* we have a strong *self-perception.* This removes the doubt factor from our minds, which keeps our thinking open and sharp rather than clouded with doubt.

We often hear people mention the need to develop skills first and then the attitude. This may work, yet we have found the attitude first provides the foundation for much quicker skill development. The mind and strong self-perception feed the need for the skills and move the skill development forward.

What do you suppose Lance Armstrong started with? Was it his vision and belief or his biking skills? Which carried him through the tough parts? If you asked him, we bet he would say his *self-perception* first, which drove his skill and endurance building.

In short, work on your *self-perception* first.

How do you really see yourself? Are you comfortable in all situations? Which are you comfortable in, which are you not? Why? This can help you sort out your strong points and indicate those areas you need to develop more. Put together a daily plan to change your *self-perception* and you will amaze yourself. Take a look in the book *Think and Grow Rich* under "auto suggestion."

To understand this concept even more, let's take a look at *self-perception*, self-confidence and the difference between them. Many people get confused and say they are the same thing, but there is a subtle yet important difference between the two.

An example might be a secretary and an executive. The secretary has a *self-perception* that she is, and can only be, a secretary. She does not see herself as a supervisor, manager and certainly not an executive. Her *self-perception* puts a ceiling on her vision of who she is or could be.

Now the executive sees himself as an executive and has taken steps to attain that level. He can move on to CEO if he truly can see himself as one.

So does this make the executive a better person than the secretary? No, it simply states this is how each person sees and limits themselves by their *self-perception*.

Does this also mean the executive has more self-confidence? No, it does not. The secretary does a great job, makes decisions quickly, is a great consensus builder within the office, is very comfortable in all her duties and people respect her. She is very self-confident.

The executive is always procrastinating on decisions, is uncomfortable with the CEO around, seems preoccupied, has to demand cooperation and is not highly regarded by his peers or subordinates. He lacks self-confidence in himself and his abilities.

Now the secretary may actually have more self-confidence and even more skills than the executive and be capable of doing a better job. But as long as she sees herself as a secretary only, nothing will change.

The executive will continue to find ways to compensate, cover up or hide his lack of self-confidence and skills so he can be the CEO. He is driven by his *self-perception*. This is how the "Peter Principle" oftentimes occurs.

> **Peter Principle:** *"A person will tend to rise to the highest level of their incompetence and stay there!"*
> - Dr. Laurence Peter

Our *self-perception* is a lot like training fleas. A flea can jump as high as three to four feet straight up. That's how they get on dogs, cats and us. They are great jumpers. To train a flea we put them in a jar and put a lid on it. Now the flea can certainly jump out of the jar with the lid off and of course tries to do so. But hitting that lid sure hurts and soon the flea is jumping just high enough so it does not hit the lid. After awhile you can take the lid off and the flea, which is completely capable of jumping out, will never leave the jar.

Our *self-perception* is like the jar lid. It can create artificial ceilings for us and our performance. There may be some effort and even some pain involved in jumping higher and through our self-imposed lids. But every one of us has the capability of doing it. To do so we need to develop the *self-perception* that sees us doing it.

Performance:

Our performance on the job and in other areas of our lives is also an outcome of this *self-perception*. Let me ask you this:

> Does your performance tend to be the same month after month?

> Do you seem to be in a comfort zone that provides you a consistent performance each month?

If you're in sales, have you had a month that looked like you were going to set a new record only to have the last week fall apart and end up at the same previous level? Have you had situations that looked like a breakthrough for you only to have something happen and bring you down to the same performance level as before?

If so, it may be that your *"self-perception* ceiling" is holding you back. Subconsciously you see yourself at a performance level of 5 on a scale of 0-10. You begin to perform at a 6 or 7 level during the month, but your *"self-perception* ceiling" says, *"You don't belong here."* Now the subconscious takes over and stupid things start happening to bring your performance down to a 5.

Review those times that seemed like you could break through and what happened to keep you from going beyond the norm. You may find that it was self-sabotage.

If this is true, what can you do to change it? Let's take a look at some of the issues we need to work with to do so.

Getting past the past:

When we look at the idea of *self-perception*, we can ask where *self-perception* comes from. Most people would agree that past experiences play a big part in how we see ourselves and where our values come from.

We all hear comments like, " *How can I do x or y when my past was such and such?* " Our response is, *"So?"* Wasn't that 20 or more years ago? We're in the *now,* talking about today and tomorrow. If we continually live today based on yesterday while trying to plan for tomorrow, we have a conflict.

Picture it this way: if we carry around a big garbage bag called *yesterday,* pile on the worries and mistakes of *today* and then add the fears of *tomorrow,* we have three large heavy garbage bags on our back. What do you suppose this does to our *self-perception?*

I recently watched a move called *Swimming Upstream.* It is based on the true story of a young boy who grew up in a poor family with a brutal older brother, a drunken, cruel father and not much hope. The father even told the boy he wished he had not been born, and this was after he had won national honors as a champion swimmer. His father had no use for the boy until he discovered his swimming ability and pushed him and his younger brother to become champions. Even then the father wanted the younger brother to be the winner and pitted the once-close brothers against each other.

In spite of all of the negative input and depressing upbringing the boy excelled and was Olympic material. In the end he made a personal choice, not based on his upbringing, not based on his father, not based on what others think or want, but on how he really wants to see himself. He had gotten past the past.

In my own life, my father also drank too much. I could never do anything right or good enough, I lost a wonderful wife in her prime and had business failures and friends and neighbors turn against me. I could have determined my *self-perception* based on those experiences. Instead, I looked at who I wanted to become and based my *self-perception* on that picture, just like the young man in the movie. Is it easy? Not really. But success often comes with a lot of hard work.

One tool that can really be of benefit here is that of forgiveness. *"What? Forgive all that bad stuff that happened to me, all that stuff others did to me?!"* The answer is *yes*. After all, who is it really hurting; them or you? Who is carrying around the garbage bag? Who is it slowing down?

In my early 20s I came to the realization that I was carrying a lot of garbage bags. When I started to simply forgive the people involved, the bags started disappearing, my mind opened up, my attitude changed and life improved drastically. If I had not forgiven and gotten rid of the garbage bags I would not have gone on to accomplish the things I have and been doing the things I am today.

Take an inventory of what motivates you and why. What are your values and what makes them your values? Then determine what baggage you need to drop to help obtain the *self-perception* you really want.

Fear

As we continue to discuss this idea of *self-perception* and how to change it, we need to talk about one four-letter word: *fear*. There is virtually no one who is totally free of fear. Each of us has to deal with some type of fear at some point in our lives.

Fear has a dramatic effect on our *self-perception*. It keeps us from believing it can be better or that we can be better or even try to be better.

Here is a short list of fears that many people cling to. You probably can add a few more to the list:

Fear of failure
Fear of success
Fear of rejection
Fear of people
Fear of change

Fear can affect our:
Self-esteem
Self-perception
Security
Ambition
Personal relationships
Ego or pride

As we look at such fears as fear of success, it really is more about fear of change of responsibility, of loss or of people. We fear the changes we have to make to our comfortable lives. We fear the responsibility that comes with success. We do not want to fail or lose what we have and we are concerned about what others might think or say. Success means we will have to change, and we may have to leave behind what is comfortable to us today. Sometimes this even means leaving some people behind.

What do we do about these fears?

First we must admit that the fears do exist, and then we must develop actions to overcome them. If one is very timid and fears people, perhaps approaching a new person every day and introducing themselves will help them overcome this fear.

If you fear speaking to a group, which is the top fear of most people, then find opportunities to speak to a small group first about something you know a great deal about. You might consider doing readings in church or offering to do small-group work in your organization or work. These will help you overcome the fear.

In some of the training we do we utilize speaking to a group as one of the tools to help instill self-confidence.

Sue was a strong-willed woman in a management position and terrified of speaking. She also had a challenge in dealing with people far too abruptly and not getting the results she wanted. The first evening she was asked to speak to a group during our training session she was visibly shaking, but she went ahead and did a good job even though she almost fainted upon sitting down. After the third time she presented, the fear had gone and you could physically see the self-confidence in her. Her *self-perception* changed and, interestingly, how she dealt with people changed as well. Sue experienced what some call a "Peak to Peek" experience.

Dr. Robert Schuler talks about "Peak to Peek" experiences. This means every time you reach a new height you get a new peek at what is on the other side. Dealing with our fears is much like that. Once we start overcoming a fear we reach a new height and get a peek at what we might be able to do.

What if you had a "Peak to Peek" experience every day?

Once you have isolated your fears, take small steps to overcome them and continue to do so until the fear is no longer an issue.

Part III:
Strategies in Creating a
New Self-Perception

Life Vision Statement

In talking about this idea of *self-perception* and how it can either propel us forward or hold us back, the question becomes, "How do we create this perception?"

Your first step is to take a good look in the mirror and ask who that person looking back really is. What could this person become? What do they want to become? A good way to start is by taking an inventory of you. What are your skills? Don't be shy or limited in noting your learned abilities. Think of everything you have ever done and the skills that were used. This alone may make a big difference in how you see yourself.

Next, take an inventory of your values. Review Section 4 to help you. Note what it is that is truly important to you. If you had to choose between one thing or another, what causes you to make the choice? What things would you do or not do? These give you clues to your values.

Now think about what has motivated you (back to Chapter 3). If money comes to mind, ask yourself what you want the money for or what it will do for you. This gets you closer to your motives.

Next, prioritize each list as to which items are the most important to you. This gives you a better look at who you are today. Now you can look and determine what, if anything, you want to change.

To start making the change, create a vivid mental picture of the changes and the type of person you want to be. It's important to not move from one view or vision until you have created a clearer one. Fear of the unknown can hold us back unless we know where we are going. Create a very vivid picture of your future that is in stark contrast to today.

Once you do, you can begin to want the future rather than the present. You are creating "cognitive dissonance," which means you have a conflict in your mind and it must be solved. Your *self-perception* begins to change and your sub-conscious mind starts creating ways to get to the new reality.

What you will create from this vision is often referred to as a "Personal Vision Statement." This is a vision or picture of what you want to become. It contains your values, self-perception and future view. Once you have a clear picture, think about how that person would act, behave and function; then begin to function that way. Creating this "vision" may take some time, yet is well worth the effort.

Affirmations

Once you have this clear *self-perception,* keep repeating positive statements and affirmations that include your strengths to help you accomplish the change. Be persistent with this; there are a lot of negatives out there to overcome.

If we could record our thoughts throughout the day and separate out how we view ourselves and then listen to it, my bet is most of us would be appalled at how negative the recording would sound. We would probably never talk to anyone else that way, yet we talk to ourselves on a daily basis using negative language. How might this be affecting our self-perception?

How do we change this "self-talk" to a more positive note? Here are a few ideas that have worked for me and others:

1. **Just be happy!** One of the most effective ways to stay positive is by being happy in the moment. This is a choice everyone has every moment of every day. Yes, all the outside people, events and issues are there, yet we can choose to be happy. Far too many people talk to themselves in this way: "I'll be happy when I am rich," or, "I'll be happy when I find the right one." They set themselves up for a bad fall when they discover happiness does not come from the outside, but from an internal choice. *Internally happy people attract the positive from the outside.*

2. **Use the word "choose" in your self-talk.** If you make a list of all the things you need to do today, this week and this month, it could easily overwhelm you: "I need to finish this project by Friday," and "I have to close five sales this week," and "I need to be a better parent."

What if you were to say it this way: "I *choose* to finish this project by Friday," and "I *choose* to close five sales this week," and "I choose to be a better parent." Does this change your feelings about what you want to accomplish? Does is make you feel less stressed and out of control?

Make a determination to "choose" your life from now on. Use the words "I choose to" in your self-talk and see what a difference it makes in how you see the world and yourself.

3. **Use presuppositions in your self-talk.** These are words that pre-suppose something is going to happen. Such words as *luckily, obviously, fortunately,*

happily, when, yet, start and *still* are examples of presuppositions.

An example of how they can be used: "Luckily in the future....." or, "Obviously you'll benefit once......" or, "When I ......" or, "Fortunately I'll ......" Thinking and self-talking in this way will keep you focused on the positive side of life.

For more on this read books such as *Think and Grow Rich*, or anything by Wayne Dwyer, Leo Buscaglia, Norman Vincent Peal and of course Zig Ziglar. Over time you will amaze yourself.

Goals:

I am sure many of you have dealt with goals, goal-setting and everything that goes with it. The question is whether or not they have worked for you.

Goals are very important and needed not only in our sales career, but in every phase of our lives. This includes our personal relationships as well.

An interesting survey was conducted in which the people were asked how important their personal relationships were. A full 99 percent said their personal relationships were the most important aspect of their lives. When asked what plans or goals they had to improve personal relationships, 100 percent said they had no such plans or goals.

Are there other important areas in our lives in which we fail to set goals? If we focus only on our business goals, are we cutting our quality of life short? If we had goals in all areas of our lives, how would it change those areas? How would that change our lives and how we view our *self-perception*?

Most have heard the analogy of a road map and how taking a vacation without a map is like living life with no goals; any road will get you there, but *where is there*? We know that goals need to be specific and measurable in some way. We know they need to have a deadline as well as a plan of action. We know we need to review them regularly and possibly even share them with others who will keep us accountable. We do all this and still the goals often don't seem to transpire.

I have found that when you work on the *self-perception* along with the goals the results are much greater. Just like our performance, goals are supported or sabotaged by our *self-perception*. So make sure your *self-perception* is in line with your goals and going in the same direction. Don't forget all the areas of your life, including your personal relationships. This will not only help you accomplish your goals but it will build your *self-perception* and round out your life.

Goals also help solve problems. How so, you ask? People often feel blocked from setting and working on goals when they feel they do not have all the information, skills or abilities needed to achieve the goal. I look at this as one more excuse not to move ahead.

The fact is that most people who achieved their goals lacked information, skills and knowledge when they first set them. One purpose of a goal is to provide the future picture. Our mind and the world around us are powerful magnets when properly focused. Dr. Wayne Dyer calls this "the source" from which all things come. Opportunities are all around us every day; we are simply not focused enough to see or attract them from "the source."

A case in point: when operating a small agricultural seed business, we needed to hit the million dollar mark. At the time we were at $250,000 and losing money. We needed a lot of assets and had not fully utilized several resources. We set the goal of $1 million in sales with a five-year plan. Although we were not sure how this would happen, we knew the number had to be hit in order for us to survive.

157

The first year we doubled the sales with some very simple ideas. We'd always had the ideas but had never pursued them until the goal created the need to think about them.

The next year we ventured way out of our comfort zone and got into exporting specialty products. In three years we were at 1.2 million in sales -- a full two years ahead of and above the goal. How and why? *Simply, goals drive creativity and problem-solving.* What do you suppose this did for our *self-perception*?

There are countless examples of people and companies having set goals that seemed out of reach, yet on the journey to that goal a completely different business developed or other opportunities were discovered. Many times these alternate opportunities turned out to be far greater and much more profitable than the original goal. Would these opportunities have occurred if the goal had not been pursued? Take a look at Thomas Edison and his story sometime. Many of his inventions occurred this way.

The next time you are contemplating a goal, don't let a lack of answers stop you. Set the goal and commit; the answers will show themselves if you are committed and looking.

Summary of Self-Perception

To help clarify the cause and effect of our self-perception, we have developed the simple diagram below.

If we start with our *self-perception* it will have an effect on our *self-image* which will affect our *self-confidence*. With a strong self, we can now carry through on our goals, which will help us find and build the skills needed.

These skills will help us get the results, which continue to build our self-perception. Thus the wheel goes round and round. We will have more "Peak to Peek" experiences and our lives will show it!

Want more Happiness in your life. Go to www.thesellinggap.com/products.html and get Vince Harris CD set on Happiness Strategies. Indicate you have "The Selling Gap" book and get 2 additional CD's on persuasion!

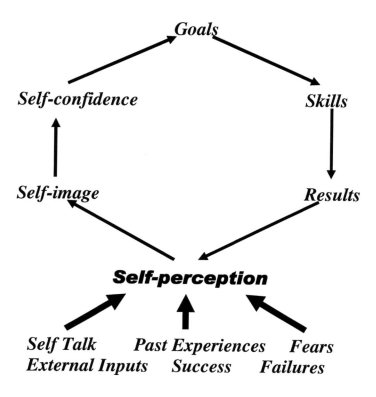

1. Self-perception is the foundation of our attitude.

2. Self-perception can propel us forward or act as a lid.

3. Self-perception can be challenging to change.

4. For us to change, our self-perception has to change

5. Self-talk and visualization are two of the most powerful ways to change.

6. Forgiveness is necessary to get rid of the garbage.

Section 8: Tying it all up

Fantastic! You have completed a study of strategies in selling. So what is your next step?

Some will simply close this book and toss it in the corner on the shelf and never look at it again. Others will contemplate the material and give some effort and attempt to apply the information and strategies they have learned. Then there are those, like you (we hope), who will pick up this book at least once per month, review it, write out your strategies on how to apply the concepts and own this material in a matter of months.

As you review each section, be aware of the personal barriers you may be experiencing or feeling as you try to apply the new concepts. Then go to Section 7 and determine which strategy and tools can help you through that barrier.

When you find yourself investing too much time in unproductive customers, review Section 2 and keep yourself on track with highly qualified customers instead. As you work to improve your selling strategies and discover a challenge in perceiving a situation, review Section 3 and 4 to refine your understanding and ability to read others and gain a better understanding of their perceptions.

If tough objections keep cropping up, or you find yourself trying to alter those beliefs that create huge walls, review Section 6 and master the objection and leading to a different conclusion process.

If getting to the core issues with your customers is the recurring challenge, review Section 4 and create better questions to help uncover larger gaps for your customers.

You realize more than anyone else that your future and success is in your hands. The tools and strategies presented here can help you accomplish your goals if you are persistent in your application of them.

So our final word to you is, set your goals, create your strategies, pick your tools and go to work.

We'll see you in the top 10 percent!

Harlan Goerger   &   Greg Deal

A Bit about Harlan & Greg

We'd like to take a few moments to introduce ourselves, your co-authors, Harlan Goerger and Greg Deal.

We're a couple of ordinary guys with some extraordinary ways of looking at life and business. We like to mix up the tried and true a bit to come up with new and more innovative, effective ways of conducting business and interacting with people, both in our work and personal lives. We are constantly researching what is working and what isn't and applying the most effective tools to real situations.

Although we began on distinctly different paths, both of us, as we ventured out into the world, ended up in the sales field. And we both found challenge rather than security to be a primary motivator in our work and lives.

Here is a little more about our backgrounds:

(Harlan) I grew up with an entrepreneurial father who started an agricultural-based seed business out of his farm. As such, I began working with customers and selling at an early age.

Eventually, I took on the entrepreneurial aspects of my father and began searching for opportunities to direct and control my destiny. Sales seemed to be the vehicle to make my dreams happen.

Early on I came upon the discovery that salespeople tended to write their own tickets and that businesses seemed to always need salespeople. Having worked in agriculture, insurance, buildings and advertising sales, I was exposed to a variety of approaches and methods of selling.

Always on the lookout for an opportunity, I successfully took a small agricultural company and, in a matter of three years, grew it 400 percent. Another entrepreneur later offered me several opportunities, one of which was corporate training. In just a few years I became a fully certified trainer and a regional manager and have since developed multiple trainers and salespeople.

After training hundreds of people and companies of all types and sizes, I began doing independent consulting. My clients have seen sales performance improvements up to 300 percent of where they began.

Today I work as president of H. Goerger & Associates Inc., out of Fargo, North Dakota, and serve as the National Director of Training for Business Architects.

 **(Greg)** I always have been intrigued by why individuals purchase products or accept ideas presented to them by others. Those curiosities lead me to a Bachelor of Science Degree in Marketing. Armed with all I needed to know (or so I thought), I went off to pursue opportunity.

As an individual desiring interaction with other people, I chose the sales profession as my ticket to paradise. Unlimited income potential, the ability to set my own hours and the chance to solve others' problems through the use of my products or services seemed greatly satisfying to me. *Warm sandy beaches here I come,* I thought.

In all honesty, I got beat up a bit in my early career. Everything mentioned above, while true, comes with a consequence for an unprepared salesperson. In addition, I didn't have a well-organized sales department, or even a sales process to fall back on; it was sink or swim.

I quickly learned that although I had the prestigious four-year college degree, I needed more education to become truly successful. So I read every book I could find on sales, including all of Og Mandino's books; subscribed to the *Success* Magazine; listened to the greats like Zig Ziglar and Tom Hopkins audio programs; and enrolled in Dale Carnegie courses taught by my co-author, Harlan. I knew I needed to gain a better understanding of the selling process, and I've never regretted taking these steps.

This strong desire to continue my understanding of sales eventually led me toward a Masters Degree in Management. That, in turn, prompted me to research what impact influence and persuasion has on one's leadership qualities, and to the discovery that gaining someone's commitment instead of just compliance can have a drastic positive effect on a leader's performance.

Sales, leadership, management and even parenting require the ability to sell (insert the word "influence") another party your ideas, product or service. Understand this concept and the world becomes your oyster.

Today, I am proud to say I am a professional salesperson. I can be anywhere and have security in my ability to provide for my loved ones and self. I enjoy my business and community endeavors, but I am a salesperson first.

(Harlan) Even with all our experience, we continue to develop our skills and understanding of sales, persuasion and personal growth on a daily basis.

And that is what this book is about: sharing the experience and knowledge we've gleaned from others to help you improve your life.

Thank you,

Harlan Goerger   &   Greg Deal

Bibliography

The Psychology of Persuasion, Kevin Hogan, Pelican Publishing

How to Win Friends and Influence People, Dale Carnegie, Simon & Schuster

One Minute Manager, Kenneth Blanchard, William Morrow

The Art of Negotiation, Herb Cohen, Bantam

Your Erroneous Zones, Wayne W. Dyer, McGraw Hill

Sales Closing Power, Douglas Edwards, Hampton House Publishing

Laws of Success, Napoleon Hill, Success Unlimited

How to Master the Art of Selling, Tom Hopkins, Warner Books

Psycho-Cybernetics, Maxwell Maltz, Wilshire Book Co.

Motivation and Personality, Abraham Maslow, Harper

Psychology of Selling, Brian Tracy, Nightengale Conant

The Psychology of Winning, Denis Waitley, Berkley

See You at the Top, Ziglar on Selling, Zig Ziglar, Ballantine

In Search of Excellence, Thomas Peters, Robert Waterman, Warner Books

The Art of Conversation, James Morris, Parker Publishing

The Way of the Bull, Leo Buscaglia, Fawcett Crest

Think and Grow Rich, Napoleon Hill, Fawcett Crest

Megatrends, John Nasibitt, Warner Books

Succeed and Grow Rich Through Persuasion, Napoleon Hill, Fawcett Crest

Tough Times Never Last But Tough People Do, Robert Schuller, Bantam Book

Success Through A Positive mental Attitude, Napoleon Hill, Simon & Schuster

Winning Strategies in Selling, Roger Staubach, Jack Kinder, Garry Kinder, Prentice-Hall

Non Verbal Selling Power, Gerhard Gschwandtner, Prentice Hall

Fundamentals of Negotiating, Gerald Nierenberg, Hawthorn/Dutton

The Great Game of Business, Jack Stack, Doubleday Currency

How to Master the Art of Selling, Tom Hopkins, Warner Books

Trout on Strategy, Jack Trout, McGraw-Hill

First Things First, Stephan Covey, Simon & Schuster

The Magic of believing, Claude Bristol, Prentice-Hall

The Art of the Deal, Donald Trump, Random House

The Renewal Factor, Robert Waterman, Bantam Books

Thriving on Chaos, Tom Peters, Alfred A. Knopf Inc.

Iacocca an Autobiography, Lee Iacocca, Bantam Books

Talking Straight, Lee Iacocca, Bantam Books

What They Don't Teach you at Harvard Business School, Mark McCormack, Bantam Books

The Golden Age, J. Paul Getty, Robert Collier Books

The Secret of the Ages, Robert Collier, Robert Collier Books

Managing Through People, Dale Carnegie & Assoc, Dale Carnegie & Assoc.

The Five Great Rules of Selling, Percy Whiting, Dale Carnegie & Assoc.

The Peter Principle, Dr. Laurence Peter, William Morrow Inc

The Best Seller, Ley Forbes

Dealing With Resistance to Persuasion, Dr. Eric Knowles DVD

Covert Persuasion, Kevin Hogan, James Speakman, Wiley Books

Influence, Robert B. Cialdini, Allyn & Bacon

Persuasion, Dave Lakhani, Wiley Books

Ask Questions, Get Sales, Stephan Schiffman, Adams Media

Prisoners of our own Beliefs, Gary Parent, Network 3000 Publishing

The Patterson Principles of Selling, Jeffrey Gitomer, Wiley Books

Changing Minds, Howard Gardner, Harvard Busines School

Contact us:

Business Architects, PO Box 5161, Fargo, ND 58105
Ph: 701-799-1972 - Email: Harlan@BusArc.com
Website:
www.BusArconline.com www.BlogBusArc.blogspot.com

Yes I am interested in additional development for my team; please contact me on the following areas:

____	Sales Training Beginner
____	Presentation Skills
____	Sales Training Experienced
____	Keynote Speakers
____	Sales Management Training
____	Short Term Workshops
____	Supervisor Management Training
____	Assessment Programs
____	Executive Coaching
____	Workshop Group
____	Customer Service Development
____	DISC Personal Style

Assessments
____	Team Building
____	360 Executive
____	Attitude and Self -Development
____	Meyers Briggs
____	Influence & Persuasion Skills

Contact Information:

Contact Name: _____
Position: _____
Company: _____
Address: _____
City: _____ State: ____Zip: _____
Dir Phone: _____

Contact us:

Business Architects, PO Box 5161, Fargo, ND 58105
Ph: 701-799-1972 - Email: Harlan@BusArc.com
Website:
www.BusArconline.com www.BlogBusArc.blogspot.com

Yes I am interested in additional development for my team; please contact me on the following areas:

____   Sales Training Beginner
____   Presentation Skills
____   Sales Training Experienced
____   Keynote Speakers
____   Sales Management Training
____   Short Term Workshops
____   Supervisor Management Training
____   Assessment Programs
____   Executive Coaching
____   Workshop Group
____   Customer Service Development
____   DISC Personal Style

        Assessments
____   Team Building
____   360 Executive
____   Attitude and Self -Development
____   Meyers Briggs
____   Influence & Persuasion Skills

Contact Information:

Contact Name: _____
Position: _____
Company: _____
Address: _____
City: _____ State: _____Zip: _____
Dir Phone: _____